Provision for Specific Learning Difficulties

by Jan Poustie

This book is dedicated to my lovely daughter Briony without whom it would never have been written.

Contents

Appendix 1

*Appendix 3
This contains the references that accompany the text in this book plus information on The *Special Educational Needs Code of Practice* (referred to in this book as COP 2002) which replaces the *Code of Practice on the Identification and Assessment of Special Educational Needs* (referred to in this book as COP 1994). Educational establishments such as LEA maintained schools, Early years settings and LEAs themselves have to a duty to 'have regard to it. They must not ignore it.' (page iii COP 2002). The differences between the two Codes of Practice are explained in Chapter 1 (also see Appendix 3).

Foreword

The Identification Solutions Library will be a valuable resource for parents, teachers and other professionals, as it clearly presents the indicators that can be observed in a range of specific learning difficulties and associated conditions.

Specialists in particular areas have been consulted and their advice, based on knowledge and experience, will certainly increase reader's understanding, making them more aware of the nature of the difficulties they are observing.

There is comprehensive information on where appropriate help, advice and diagnosis can be obtained. This, in itself, will relieve many anxieties – to take a book from a shelf and find a possible solution to problems will, hopefully, ensure that children and adults get the right help at the right time.

Violet Brand

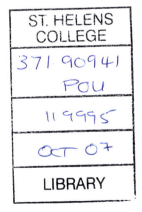
Acknowledgements

Grateful thanks go to:

Dr Peter Gardner, Chartered Educational psychologist and co-founder of Appleford School,

Violet Brand, International speaker on dyslexia,

Carol Orton, Ex-Befriender Coordinator, British Dyslexia Association.

Members of the **SENCO-forum** internet group who have contributed to this book. (See page 24).

Many thanks go to the following agencies and organisations, and their staff:

- The College of Speech and Language Therapists,
- Various departments/members of OFSTED,
- The Department for Education and Skills,
- Special Educational Needs Tribunal,
- Schools Curriculum and Assessment Authority,
- National Association for Gifted Children,
- CLASS,
- Her Majesty's Inspectorate of Prisons,
- Local Government Ombudsman.

Many thanks to the various organisations that gave me permission to quote from their publications. "Crown copyright is produced with the permission of the controller of Her Majesty's Stationery Office." My thanks also to family, friends and colleagues who have supported and encouraged me along the way.

The views expressed by the author are her own and do not necessarily represent those who have contributed to, or assisted with, the writing of this library.

Jan Poustie

Using the Identification Solutions for Specific Learning Difficulties Library

Professionals and parents have contacted me over the years to thank me for writing the original book *Solutions for Specific Learning Difficulties: Identification Guide* upon which this library is based. Through its information they have been able to make accurate and reliable identifications and provide/obtain appropriate provision. I wanted to make this edition much easier to use and so now I have divided the information into separate books and included identification checklists in each of them. There are various ways to use this library, all of which involve starting at page v to gain an overview of the Specific Learning Difficulties Profile. Many will find that pages vi to x offer valuable insights into provision. After that you can:

→→ Read each book in the library, or

→→ Start at the book, or chapter within it, which interests you most, or

→→ Fill in the checklists in this book, and then read the relevant chapters or books from this library as indicated.

This library has been designed for individuals to 'find' the elements of the picture and then know to whom to go for diagnosis, help and support. Many indicators can be found in more than one condition so if a common indicator is present you may find yourself being directed to look at several parts of the library. (It is not the isolated indicator that you need to look for in a condition but the whole picture. If you want your identification to be more reliable you should not just look at the checklists and/or the index. Instead you should look at the relevant books of the library which will refer you to different parts of the library and so the 'whole' picture will emerge. You will usually 'know' when the full picture has emerged as it will 'feel right and complete'.)

Many who read this library may have one or two of the indicators for a particular condition but this does not necessarily mean that they have the condition itself. (It's a bit like a sneeze does not mean that you have flu!). However, whilst reading through this library, some of you may realise that it is likely that you (the parent/adult/professional) and/or your child have the conditions that come within (or are associated with) the SpLD Profile. For some of you it might explain much of what has happened in the past and what is happening now, and for some that may seem quite devastating and be a very traumatic experience. If this is the case, it is important to remember that there has been no change in you and/or your child since you picked up this book - just a change in your perception. There is a network of help, support, advice, assessment and intervention available to you which the books in this library will help you to find and access. The information that you gain from the library will not, in itself, fulfil your hopes, dreams and aspirations, but it may be the first step towards their realisation.

Jan

You may find it helpful to have a piece of paper handy to write down the Book/ chapter numbers as you are referred to them. Once you have read all the relevant sections of the library, you must decide which of the difficulties is causing the most problem. Arrange a referral for that area first, but remember that it can take months before an individual is seen.

Please do not wait until a diagnosis has been made before contacting your relevant local help and support groups – they exist just for you, whether you are a parent, teenager, adult or professional. (They will not think that you have wasted their time if assessment shows that the individual does not have the condition.) See Appendix 2.

The Specific Learning Difficulties Profile

The following conditions can be seen as part of the SpLD Profile:

Specific Language Impairment (usually known as dysphasia in adults) A continuum of difficulties experienced by children and young people who have not reached expected competence in communication skills in their first language, and whose teaching and learning is consequently affected. The condition causes difficulties with expressive language (that which you speak or write) and receptive language (that which you hear or read). Often this group is defined by exclusion: 'They are not autistic, the impairment is not the result of a physical, intellectual or hearing impairment.' (Norma Corkish, ex-Chief Executive, AFASIC)

Dyscalculia
Developmental Dyscalculia: Difficulties in understanding, processing and using numerical/mathematical information. It is often accompanied by one or more of the other conditions found within the Specific Learning Difficulty Profile. The identification, assessment and management of Dyscalculia is a huge topic. So, the information on Dyscalculia that was originally in the first edition of this book has now been transferred and vastly extended to form another title. Readers interested in this topic should access *Mathematics Solutions – An Introduction to Dyscalculia: Parts A and B* by Jan Poustie (published by Next Generation).

Autistic Spectrum Disorder: (used to be called Autistic Continuum): Difficulties in social interaction, social communication and imagination-based activities/behaviour.

Central Auditory Processing Disorder: A dysfunction of the processing of auditory input causing problems with understanding/ processing what is heard.

Attention Deficit Disorder: (also known as Attention Deficit Hyperactivity Disorder and Behaviour Inhibition Disorder): Causes difficulties in concentrating/focusing attention and memorising information. It affects behaviour and has several forms.

Dyspraxia (also known as Developmental Dyspraxia. Other terms used for coordination difficulties are Developmental Coordination Disorder (DCD), sensory integration problems, coordination difficulties and motor-learning problems): There are various forms, all of which relate to difficulties in motor planning and organisation. It can affect the ability to cope with sensory stimuli; perceptual difficulties are likely to be present too. It can affect speech, eye, limb, body, hand and finger movements.

Dyslexia (also known as Developmental Dyslexia): In the past, this has been used as an umbrella term for several of the conditions found within the SpLD Profile. Nowadays, it is more appropriate to use this term only in respect of a condition where the main difficulties are with the acquisition and use of spelling and/or reading skills.

Various other conditions are associated with the conditions found within the Specific Learning Difficulties Profile such as:
▸▸ Meares-Irlen Syndrome (see Book 4 of the library),
▸▸ CFS/ME (see Book 1 of the library),
▸▸ Metabolic Dysfunctioning (see Book 1 of the library),
▸▸ Childhood Hemiplegia (see Book 1 of the library).

The stages of the Special Needs Code of Practice
(Also see page 2 and Appendix 3.)

The *Special Educational Needs Code of Practice* (referred to in this book as COP 2002) came into force in England on 1st January 2002. (For information on other parts of the UK see Appendix 3). COP 2002 replaced the code that had been published in 1994 (referred to in this book as COP 1994). Professionals and parents can obtain a free copy of the COP 2002 and the SEN Toolkit (ISBN 1 84185 531 6) which accompanies it by ringing 0845 6022260. Alternatively the Code can be found on the website of the Department for Education and skills: www.dfes.gov.uk/sen

COP 1994 had a Stage 1, there is no equivalent stage in COP 2002. In COP 2002 Early Years/School Action is roughly equivalent to Stage 2 of COP 1994, Early Years/School Action Plus is roughly equivalent to Stage 3 of COP 1994.

COP 1994, Stage 2/COP 2002, School Action

COP 1994, Stage 2

The AENCO/SENCO took the lead in assessing the child's learning difficulties, planning, monitoring/reviewing the special educational provision, working with the child's teachers and ensuring that the child's parents were consulted.

COP 2002, School Action

The names of students who are at this stage (or are at later stages; e.g. Action Plus or who are Statemented) should be kept on a SEN register which is kept by the SENCO. Students will move on to this stage if they are not making adequate progress.[1] Primary schools may use the National Literacy Strategy (NLS) and the National Numeracy Strategy (NNS) objectives as the criteria for deciding which stage the student is at; e.g. a Year-6 child working at a Year-4 literacy objective might be placed at School Action. In the case of complex SpLD Profile conditions such as Dyspraxia, the most noticeable area of learning difficulty may have already been recognised/assessed by School Action but no one may have yet made the connection with Dyspraxia. Unless a multidisciplinary assessment is made at the outset it will often be the most noticeable area of difficulty that is assessed first, with later assessments being made as the 'whole picture' of the child emerges.

COP 1994, Stage 3/COP 2002, School Action Plus (SAP/SA+)

COP 1994, Stage 3

The school called upon external specialist support to help the pupil to make progress.

COP 2002, School Action Plus (SAP/SA+)

The school is expected to ask for information from outside

A new Code of Practice for Wales (largely the same as the English version but including guidance for the assessment of bi-lingual children) was published in the Spring of 2002. For more information, contact the Education department in the National Assembly of Wales, Tel: 02920 826081 or go to their website: www.wales.gov

professionals at any of the COP stages; e.g. initially seeking informal advice from their LEA's Special Needs Support Team or other professionals who already work within the school, such as paediatric occupational/physio/speech and language therapists. By the time a child reaches SAP the parent may already have made direct referrals (and received assessments) via a doctor for motor, speech and language difficulties.

COP 1994, Stage 4/COP 2002, Referral for a Statutory Assessment

COP 1994, Stage 4
Referral for a statutory assessment.

COP 2002, Referral for a Statutory Assessment
The LEA, in cooperation with those concerned with the child (parents and professionals), considers whether a statutory multidisciplinary assessment should be made (see Book 1 and page 16 for details). If it decides to assess, then the LEA has to seek, in writing, parental, educational, medical, psychological, and social services advice, plus any other views (including those of the child) that are regarded as being desirable. If the LEA refuses to make an assessment/award a Statement of Special Educational Needs, then an appeal (to the Special Educational Needs Tribunal) can be made against the decision no matter who (school, nursery providers or child's guardians) made the original request for the assessment (see page 16).

COP 1994, Stage 5/COP 2002, Statements of Special Educational Needs

COP 1994, Stage 5
The issuing of a Statement of Special Educational Needs.

New COP, Statements of Special Educational Needs
The issuing of a Statement of Special Educational Needs occurs. It 'should specify clearly the provision necessary to meet the needs of the child. It should detail appropriate provision to meet each identified need.'[4] 'Provision should normally be quantified (e.g. in terms of hours of provision, staffing arrangements). ... It will always be necessary for LEAs to monitor ... the child's progress towards identified outcomes. ... LEAs must not, in any circumstances, have blanket policies not to quantify provision.'[5] 'LEAs should also set out ... any disapplications or modifications of the provisions of the National Curriculum (... attainment targets, programmes of study and assessment arrangements) which they consider necessary to meet the child's special educational needs. ... Where pupils are educated at home by their parents there is no requirement to deliver the National Curriculum.'[6]

COP 2002, Referral for a Statutory Assessment
The assessment should take into account the fact that 'medical conditions may have a significant impact on a child's experiences and the way they function in school. The impact may be direct in that the condition may affect cognitive or physical abilities, behaviour or emotional state. The impact may also be indirect, perhaps disrupting access to education through unwanted effects of treatment or the psychological effects which serious or chronic illness or disability can have on a child and their family.'[2] It is essential that there should be 'consultation and open discussion between' various bodies; e.g. the child's parents, the child's GP, the community paediatrician and any specialist services providing treatment for the child to 'ensure that the child makes maximum progress.'[3]

Provision for Specific Learning Difficulties by Jan Poustie   ISBN 1 901544 18 4

A word from the author

Many adults are defeated in their desire to obtain academic success because of the presence of the SpLD Profile conditions. I was lucky, yes, it was a huge struggle but I did manage to gain my degree. As a mother of two gifted daughters (who both have a range of SpLD Profile conditions) I realised early on that appropriate and effective provision was dependent upon accurate identification of the conditions. After spending six years researching my children's difficulties (and ways of overcoming them) I realised that if professionals, parents (and adults who have the conditions) were to have a chance of making a full identification of the problems then everyone needed to have the information that I had acquired.

By 1996 my younger daughter was in great distress on a daily basis, her specific learning difficulties were neither accepted nor provided for by her school. This led me to writing the original 'Gaining Provision' chapter which was published in the first edition of this library in 1997 under the title *Solutions for Specific Learning Difficulties: Identification Guide*. Thanks to my special needs teaching background (and the knowledge I had gained via my research) I was able to teach my daughter to read and spell despite the severity and range of her difficulties. Unable, even with the intervention of the Local Education Authority (LEA), to persuade her primary school to accept (or provide appropriately for) her difficulties I was forced to move her to another primary school which had a specialist SpLD teacher. Within this supportive environment her literacy skills improved; though, as Winnie the Pooh would say, her spelling is still a bit 'wobbly'. Since the age of eleven years she has thirstily read her way through my science fiction library (I have to admit to being a 'Trekkie' and a Star Wars fan).

My daughter achieved success because her provision matched her needs. Many feel threatened as soon as the word 'provision' is mentioned. Parents who understand the conditions want provision and want it now. Many of them fear that their children will follow the same path as themselves, struggle to acquire qualifications and have difficulties in developing relationships or achieving a worthwhile career. The earlier we provide appropriate provision the better result we will have. At an early stage we can provide efficiently and effectively for our students for a relatively small outlay of time and money (compared to the cost if we delay). Some students will require the use of specialist materials in small group settings whilst others will require specialist 1:1 intervention. The first level of provision is not complicated. It is achieved by changing our perception of the SpLD Profile conditions and how they impact on the student. This, in turn, leads us to change our attitudes and teaching methods (including teaching to the student's natural learning style) and to make simple adjustments within the classroom. Even the next level of provision has been made easier for us thanks to some superb computer software and good quality materials

The professional/parent may not be able to see the condition. How much simpler it would be if our SpLD students had green skin, purple antennae or even just a plaster cast on their legs. These things we would all be able to instantly recognise, there would be no problem in achieving an identification and diagnosis. Unfortunately, the real world is not so simple. We have the task of spotting the conditions no matter how well masked they are by factors such as high intelligence, social deprivation and a student who struggles to show that s/he can cope and that s/he is not different from the others in the class.

for both teachers and students. When receiving this level of provision we would expect the school-aged child to be entered as being at Early Years Action or School Action under the *Special Educational Needs Code of Practice* (COP 2002). If we want to achieve the best outcome, the student's needs have to be addressed early on, especially early in the primary school (or as early as possible once s/he has transferred to a new educational setting; e.g. moved to secondary school).

We can ignore or pay lip-service to our SpLD students but this road leads to them rejecting us just as we have rejected them. This (along with the other factors mentioned in Book 1 of this library and in the conclusion of this book) may lead to behavioural problems in and out of the classroom. Failure to provide adequately for the student leads to great stress and distress for the student, the parents (or the adult student's family) and to the educational professionals themselves. This results in disillusionment for all the parties concerned; if allowed to continue then the future becomes bleak. The longer the situation continues the less faith the parents and students will have that the educational system cares (or indeed that the professionals are competent). LEA professionals can either be life-savers in this nightmare scenario or can make the situation even worse.

Sometimes the system works. Appropriate provision is given without the parent having to struggle to obtain it. When a Statement of Special Educational Needs is needed (in order to gain very specialist provision) it is made without the parents having to fight for it. However, for far too many children that is not the case. Many parents may be told that their child cannot be statemented as s/he is not in the bottom two per cent of the child population for literacy/numeracy skills etc. However, two per cent as the upper limit seems nonsensical as, at the end of 2001, three per cent of the child population held statements. (See John Howson's report in the Times Educational Supplement dated 02/11/01.) Some LEAs are reducing the number of (or disbanding) their specialist SpLD teachers/advisors. In such cases, schools are expected to buy in such specialist services. However, some LEAs have devolved their Special Educational Needs (SEN) budget. This means that the school has control over it and not the LEA; this can result in the school deciding to spend the SEN money on non-SEN purposes. The only way to overcome this problem is for the LEA to ring-fence the SEN budget so that schools can only use it for the purpose for which it was intended.

Throughout the rough and stony road of trying to gain provision the behaviour of all parties (professionals and parents) can deteriorate. Class and head teachers can become hostile to the parent and the student. The support some parents and students receive from professionals is exceptional whilst others attempt to protect their backs (or the interests of the LEA or the school) whilst ignoring, or paying lip-service to, the interests of the child. I, like many parents (and adult SpLD Profile individuals) have found that the cost of failure to provide appropriately has been very high. (Many parents have to take out second mortgages to afford the lessons, assessments and appeals

Professionals may see issues such as class sizes, government league tables, National Curriculum demands, funding and just sheer lack of energy and time as being the obstacles to achieving appropriate and effective provision for our SpLD students. Some people go into denial when confronted with an SpLD student. One, or more, of the parents may not be able to accept that this 'chip off the old block' has the SpLD Profile. Parents may have to face the reality that they too have the conditions and that their children have inherited their difficulties. Alongside the parents' acceptance must come action, liaison with professionals plus an understanding of the conditions and how they affect the student both at school and at home. The need to do all of this can put a great strain on the parents.

Chronic Fatigue Syndrome/ Myalgic Encephalomyelitis/Post Viral Fatigue Syndrome (CFS/ ME/PVFS).

This condition (especially in its moderate to severe forms) can cause an acquired form of many of the SpLD Profile conditions. The huge lack of knowledge of this condition has created great problems for many parents and their CFS/ME children, especially as there are no tests currently available to prove that the condition is present. This has resulted in parents (especially of children who are severely affected by CFS/ME) being open to accusations of child abuse; some have had their children taken away from them. The new Chief Medical Officer's report on CFS/ME (published 2002, available from the Department of Health) contains advice for professionals to stop this professional abuse of parents and children happening in the future.

to the SEN Tribunal.) The stress, distress, cost in man hours and impact upon family resources (emotional and financial) has been huge during my nine year struggle to obtain appropriate provision for my youngest daughter. In my family's case it has resulted in a great deterioration in my daughter's health during the past few months and myself becoming ill through stress. Some marriages cannot take the stress and the couple breaks up. Some students cannot cope and commit suicide.

Once trust between the parties no longer exists then trust becomes replaced by fear. Many SpLD Profile parents are fearful. They fear that if they keep on asking for provision the educators will become angry and take out their anger on the child. Five years ago, the bulk of my daughter's SpLD problems had been overcome (she has both Dyslexia and Occulomotor Dyspraxia). Then she became ill with Chronic Fatigue Syndrome/Myalgic Encephalomyelitis (CFS/ME) which causes an acquired form of the SpLD Profile. For the next five years I lived in fear that if I complained too loudly about what was happening educationally to my severely ill daughter then one professional or another (medical or educational) would claim that she did not have CFS/ME and my daughter would be taken away from me. Frightened parents often ask for very little for fear of making the situation worse. Over a period of years I asked for basic things; e.g. ramps for her wheelchair, for her form room to remain downstairs rather than be moved upstairs and finally for GCSE mathematics tuition. As each request was denied, my daughter and I became more and more distressed, and (like many other parents and students) we lost faith in the school and the LEA. Eventually we were no longer even being informed of changes in the times of her lessons (especially important as she only attended school for four lessons a week). The relationship between parent and school soured and communication between ourselves and the school ground to a halt.

Many parents of SpLD Profile children are in a situation where some or all of the teachers do not accept that the SpLD profile conditions are present. Therefore the professionals do not assess or refer the child for assessment, nor do they provide for the conditions. This situation can occur because of lack of training. (Our teacher training colleges provide very little training in specific learning difficulties and some cannot recognise the conditions in their own students!) Some teachers (unaware of paras. 5:2 and 6:2 in the Code of Practice) may feel that the learning support department/SENCO are responsible for special needs provision and not themselves (see Appendix 3).

Fearing that my daughter's school did not believe the severity of her illness I tried to retrieve the situation by calling a multidisciplinary meeting of all those involved with my daughter. The meeting confirmed my fears. My daughter was now in great distress and I was terrified that she would be taken away from me. I realised that her education needed protecting via a statement. So, for the third time in her life, I asked an LEA educational psychologist (EP) about the chance of her being awarded one and again was told it was unlikely. However, a few months earlier I had spoken to a member of an OFTSED inspection team. He had told me that he was astonished that my daughter (who had only attended school for one lesson a day for four days of the week for a period of five years) did not have a Statement. I therefore, decided to ignore the EP's advice and applied to the LEA for a statutory assessment for her.

Once the situation becomes a battle many parents of SpLD children (or adults with the conditions themselves) have to seek outside specialist help; e.g. educational/medical assessments. In my case I needed a specialist consultant pediatrician to confirm the diagnosis of CFS/ME and to write a report advising the LEA (and the school) how to proceed educationally with my child. By now I was ill with stress and my child had relapsed. (She was continuously being wracked by muscle spasms and her fatigue was so great that I now had to wash and dress her.) Despite all of this we made the journey to the other end of the country to see the specialist who then wrote the report. Last month I learned that the LEA will be making a statutory assessment of my daughter.

Now, my daughter is functioning at 20% of normal, just fifteen minutes of studying causes her condition to worsen for about four hours at a time; e.g. she has pain and muscle spasms plus language, visual and reading skills deteriorate. An EP assessment could cause her to relapse further so it will need to be conducted by an EP who is a specialist in CFS/ME. (The seriousness of very severe CFS/ME is often not realised; some people are bed-ridden for years and some have to be tube fed for months).

Parents and students who lose faith in those who are meant to provide may decide to go to court. Many schools and LEAs are at risk of being sued and in the future there may be a risk that individual teachers will be held responsible and may find themselves being taken to court too. Legal cases in the past indicate that the best way to avoid this happening is to do the following:

- Accept advice (and act upon expressions of concern) from qualified professionals even if they are not those that the organisation normally uses. Educators can contact organisations such as the British Dyslexia Association and the Dyspraxia Foundation for a list of appropriate qualifications. If the government feels that external evidence can be accepted when deciding whether to make a statutory assessment (see para. 7:35 Code of Practice) then it must also be accepted during the rest of the child's educational career.
- Do not by your actions cause distress to the child and his/her parents/carers.
- Do not lose the trust of the parents/carers.
- Keep the parents/carers informed of all changes in provision and advise them as soon as there is reason for concern.
- Put everything in writing and where possible obtain a signature

Failure on the LEA's part to ensure that their own guidelines are being used by their schools and the tactics used by some to avoid Statementing children put both the child and the family under severe pressure. Some LEAs appear to have made brinkmanship into an art when a parent is desperately trying to negotiate the turbulent waters of trying to obtain a Statement. The LEA staff would not have endured months of distress before they agreed at long last to make a Statement but the parent has. The parent (and indeed the whole of the student's family) can be traumatised by the whole process of trying to gain provision.

The conditions in this book affect many individuals, regardless of their race, colour or creed. For some of them, daily tasks can be likened to running a marathon without any equipment, training or strategies. Some cannot maintain the willpower they need to succeed and so they start to fail. The more they fail, the lower their self-esteem. The lower their self-esteem, the more anxious they become about their difficulties (and the less inclined to attempt the task because they now expect to fail). If we, as a society, fail our SpLD students then we determine society's own fate. We will see increasing numbers who, because of poor basic skills, cannot become employed. Some will find themselves so disenchanted with our society that they may travel on a one-way path to prison (see page 42 for further details).

from the carer/parent so that you have proof that they have seen the document.

Of great concern to many of us are the behavioural problems that are now beginning to overwhelm our schools. Such problems may mask the underlying causes, including the fact that the diet may be lacking in important elements; e.g. essential fatty acids or that it has too much of certain items; e.g. sugar, saturated fats and caffeine (see Appendix 3 plus Books 1 and 5). There is also a growing body of evidence that mental functioning can be improved by vitamin and mineral supplementation (see pages 146 - 152, *The Optimum Nutrition Bible* by Patrick Holford, ISBN 0749918551).

Identification (leading to the diagnosis) of a difficulty can be the first step towards success. This leads to the second step – making appropriate provision to help students gain the skills needed to achieve their goals (strategies to achieve this can be found in other Next Generation titles; e.g. *Literacy Solutions*, *Mathematics Solutions: an Introduction to Dyscalculia* and *Planning and Organisation Solutions*). Often, diagnosis starts the 'raising of self-esteem', which is an essential part of provision for the difficulties. Diagnosis provides an explanation for the failure – the individual no longer has to feel inadequate, s/he is not lazy, careless and a failure. If we provide appropriate and effective provision for our SpLD students we have a chance of reducing the number of SpLD individuals in prison and reducing the number of those who are alienated from our society and/or who fail to achieve their potential. The *HM Prison Service Annual Report and Accounts* (April 2000 – March 2001) states that it costs £27,636 to maintain a prisoner for a year (plus there is the human cost of the emotional trauma of the prisoner, the family and the victim). A much better use of that money would be to fund a full-time specialist SpLD teacher for a year! The future does not have to be bleak. The attempt to gain provision does not have to be a battle for parents, students and professionals. The whole process need not be destructive, it can be constructive for as my daughter says:

> We should not be thinking in terms of a battle to gain provision. Instead we should be thinking of building a tower together, the top of the tower will be my provision.

This library has been written to help change the future for our SpLD students, the parents of our SpLD Profile children and the professionals who educate and care for them. If we believe in our ability to help these students, and accept the need for cooperation between all of the parties involved with the student, then together we can achieve success.

Jan Poustie

CHAPTER 1
Provision

This Chapter concentrates on children because they are the majority of those being assessed and provided for. Some private tutors and organisations; e.g. the Dyslexia Institute (Tel. 01784 463 851), assess both adults and children. Adults who want a referral for a speech and language assessment can either make a direct referral to their local Speech and Language Therapy Service or ask their GP to make the referral for them. The Information Office of The Royal College of Speech and Language Therapists can provide details of your local Speech and Language Therapy service. (7 Bath Place, Rivington Street, London EC2A 3DR, Tel: 0171 6133855, Fax: 0171 6136413.)

PART 1 – The Code of Practice
All references in this chapter and chapter 2 have been placed in Appendix 3 (see page 9).

The way in which the Department for Education and Skills recommends that assessment and provision should be carried out for pupils with special educational needs in England and Wales is laid out in its Code of Practice (COP) – see Chapter 2. We are now at a period of transition, as the government has replaced the COP that was issued in 1994 (COP 1994) with a new one (COP 2002).

Resolving disagreements about provision
The *Special Educational Needs Code of Practice 2002* (COP 2002) introduces 'Disagreement Resolution Services' (DRS) which all LEAs must provide. It is hoped that these will reduce the number of appeals going to the SEN Tribunal. The aim is that the service can be used before going to Appeal (or whilst an Appeal is in progress) and that it will provide an informal resolution of disagreements.[1]
The idea of providing an informal mediation service is a good one. There is great emphasis in the COP 2002 on the importance of an effective partnership between the LEA, school and parents and the need for transparent polices on the part of the LEA.[2] The government does not expect there to be a need for legal representation when using DRS.[3] Historically, however, some LEAs and schools have not been transparent in their policies nor have they regarded parents as equal partners. In some areas of the country it will be a 'tall order' indeed to turn this situation around. Thus, unfortunately, since parents can feel highly intimidated when faced by a group of professionals, it would seem likely that legal/professional representation will be sought by some of them for such mediation meetings.

The availability of local assessment/provision for adults may be different across the UK, as it is dependent upon what the Local Authority has contracted the service to provide. An adult's GP can refer him/her to physio/occupational therapists for assessments. Adults who are looking for assessment/provision can obtain advice from The Dyspraxia Foundation's adult helpline, Tel: 0207 7435 5443 and from the Adult Dyslexia Organisation, Tel: 0207 7377646. *Developmental Dyspraxia* by Madeleine Portwood (pub. David Fulton Publishers) contains a motor screening assessment tool that can be used with adults.

The COP 2002 has a much greater emphasis on parental and student involvement with regards to provision including the importance of:

- ▸▸ all students (including the very young) being involved in the decision-making process,
- ▸▸ preventing a deterioration in the relationship between the school/LEA and the parents.

The Code of Practice (COP)

Most of the COP 2002 is an ADVISORY document. It provides guidance to educational establishments and LEAs as to how they should manage special needs provision. Only certain sections of it (which can be found in specially highlighted boxes) must be implemented. The COP 2002 works in the same way no matter which condition is present. There is an expectation that parents will be kept informed at all stages and that the views of the child will be taken into consideration when deciding provision. The SENCO (Special Educational Needs Coordinator) also known in some schools as the AENCO (Additional Educational Needs Coordinator), manages the SEN provision in schools (see pages 39-40 Glossary of terms).

Students do not have to pass through all of the COP 2002 stages, they can move directly to Referral for a Statutory Assessment. Relatively little training in COP 2002 will have taken place prior to it coming into force in 2002 because the substantial revisions to the document (which caused its publication to be delayed by over a year) has meant that no-one could be certain of its contents until late 2001. This will result in a most unsatisfactory situation for both professionals and parents since teachers will have to put into practice the recommendations of a document about which they may know very little.

Differences between COP 1994 and COP 2002
Also see pages vi-vii and Appendix 3

The five stage assessment process of COP 1994 has been replaced by four stages in COP 2002. Many students will enter the first two stages (School Action/Early Years Action and School Action Plus/Early Years Action Plus) but very few will move on to the final two stages of Statutory Assessment and making a Statement of Special Educational Needs. From the parental point of view there are some very important changes. For example, under Stage 1 of COP 1994 we had the AENCO/SENCO entering the child on to an SEN Register following identification of initial concern. Information was then gathered, early action taken if necessary within the normal classroom work and progress was monitored and reviewed. Under COP 2002 this stage no longer exists. Although theoretically there is no need to maintain an SEN register of students at this point the wise AENCO/SENCO will keep a list of such students and any action taken; e.g. monitoring of progress, meetings with parents.

PART 2 - Provision

Qualifications of the providers

There are various professionals who are qualified to provide for the conditions found within the SpLD Profile. Local professionals with an interest/expertise in this field can be found via the local groups of the national organisations found in Appendix 2. Specialised medical staff, such as occupational/physio therapists and doctors, have *paediatric* qualifications. Teaching staff may hold a variety of qualifications. (The British Dyslexia Association hold a list of Accredited teachers who have appropriate qualifications. Individuals with the highest qualifications and breadth of experience can write AMBDA after their name.) Ideally, SpLD students should receive their provision from specialist teachers/ LSAs. The latter may have the Certificate for Classroom Assistants in Specific Learning Difficulties and hold an ALSA (Accredited Learning Support Assistants) which is awarded by the British Dyslexia Association (Tel. 0118 9668271). Some medical professionals may also hold qualifications that are normally held by teachers; for example, the RSA/OCR Dip. SpLD. Some courses leading to specialist educational qualifications concentrate on literacy difficulties. So, if students have a non-literacy based condition it is important to check whether the professional has a good knowledge of the type of provision that is required.

Dependent upon the knowledge/experience of the teachers, state schools should be able to provide for individuals with low-level forms of the conditions found within the SpLD Profile. Moderate and severe difficulties (or students with very complex profiles) are likely to need specialist input from an LEA Special Needs Support Team (SENST), or by suitably qualified specialist teachers (who may be employed by the school or paid for privately) or by a school that specialises in the particular condition/s. In some cases, there can be difficulties in gaining provision (see Chapter 2). The local organisers of the various national agencies may be able to advise on local private/state provision (see the Help and Support sections in each book of this library). *Which School for Special Needs* (edited by D. Bingham) and the free CReSTed booklet (see page 16), provide useful lists of specialist schools (see Help and Support for details).

Assessment

Educational assessment:

This usually includes a mixture of formal and informal tests and, in the case of children, classroom observation. The assessment 'tools' (tests, diagnostic/identification checklists etc.) used are determined by the professional's qualifications. Most teachers have had little or no training in assessment (and some may not know enough about child

Support

LEAs advise schools as to the criteria that the student has to meet to be on each stage of the COP. As this criteria varies substantially across the UK a child moving from one LEA to another (or even from one school to another in the same LEA) could be put at a different stage and receive very different provision. There is already evidence that some LEAs are advising schools to provide an amount of support worked out according to a formula rather than based upon the exact needs of the students; e.g. five hours support a week for *School Action* students and nine hours for *School Action Plus* students. Some totally inappropriate practices exist. The author knows of an incident where an LEA psychologist went into a school and told the staff to demote all children on the SEN register by one level! Unfortunately, one fears that such bad practice will continue to happen.

Medical assessment
The assessor/s will recommend various activities and strategies that may help the individual; many of which can be carried out in the classroom and/or home. The individual with moderate/severe difficulties is likely to require specialist intervention, which may take place in school, in a speech and language/physio/occupational therapy unit, or in the home.

development). There is a move to more informal assessments (for example, observation of the student). This change is partly due to concerns as to whether IQ tests are meaningful; it also reflects the great shortage of educational psychologists and other assessors, such as those who hold an OCR/RSA SpLD Diploma.

Reports
When discussing provision with staff, parents should not assume that the school has a copy of the report, even though they may have been sent one. It can be lost in the post or within the school itself, especially when a number of people have access to it. Never send originals of reports to the school/LEA, always send a copy.)

PART 3 – Should we use labels?

There is much discussion amongst professionals, and those who have the SpLD Profile conditions, as to whether one should 'label' the individual by stating the conditions that are present. Some parents/individuals feel relief when they can give a name to the difficulties, whilst others feel that such labelling is inappropriate. Some parents/adults are resentful if not told the name of the condition and feel that the professional is 'hiding' the condition from them (or has been inefficient and failed to recognise it). Many professionals feel that too much importance is given to the label; in other words it is not the condition but the provision for it that matters. Some may be reluctant to name the condition for fear of mis-diagnosing or because they cannot, at this stage, make a clear-cut diagnosis. Still other professionals are aware that some parents may not be ready to face the long-term implications of particular conditions, for example, Autistic Spectrum Disorder, and so may be reluctant to name them. (Parents may also refuse to tell their child that s/he has a SpLD Profile condition.)

There are several good reasons for giving the individual/parent a name for the condition. Individuals are unlikely to find a book about it in a library unless they know what the condition is called. Labels make it easier to know which of the specialist agencies could help; for example, The Dyspraxia Foundation. Labels can also help in identifying the academic and social needs of a particular individual. They help us to understand, tolerate and make allowances for the behaviours that can be found as part of the condition; for example, the clinging/'personal-space-invading behaviour' of some children who have Dyspraxia and the child with Dyslexia who always lays the table incorrectly. The arguments over the labelling issue will no doubt always be with us – perhaps we have to acknowledge that this is one case where there is unlikely to be a solution!

CHAPTER 2
Gaining Provision

For convenience and ease of understanding of the complex area of provision the parent is referred to as 'she', the teacher as 'he' and the child as 'he'. The author is aware that SpLD affects both sexes, that both parents can be involved in gaining provision for their child and that teachers who have to face these difficulties are of both sexes. All footnotes relate to the Code of Practice 2002 (COP 2002), which replaced the 1994 COP during 2002. The paragraphs of this document that references relate to (and information on this document) can be found in Appendix 3.

The gaining of provision for a child may be swift and easy, very slow, or may not be achieved at all. There are pockets of excellent practice within the schools of Britain. In some cases, a parent needs only to express her concern for this to be acted upon, assessments made and appropriate provision provided. Unfortunately, this is not always the case and sometimes this occurs because the child's form of Specific Learning Difficulty is so deeply hidden.

Various factors can hide the SpLD Profile. These include:

→ Superior intellectual ability masking the difficulties. (Thus the child is seen to be working at the average level of ability, his superior intellectual ability is not apparent, and therefore teaching staff feel there is no cause for concern.)

→ Difficulties within the family situation, such as a divorce, can mask the learning difficulty. (The teaching staff believe that emotional problems to do with home are causing the child to react in an emotional way; e.g. being anxious, misbehaving, daydreaming etc. and so they do not 'see' the SpLD.)

→ The child being mislabelled by educators as being spoilt/ misbehaving rather than having a condition such as Attention Deficits. This condition affects the child's behaviour and the way in which he concentrates and focuses attention. (This condition has many effects, such as impulsiveness in speech and/or behaviour, daydreaming, sleeping problems and so on. The non-hyperactive form of this condition may be easily missed by teaching staff.)

The child could be affected by one of the lesser known forms of Specific Learning Difficulty, such as:

→ **Dyspraxia, (also known as Developmental Coordination Disorder, DCD)** which has wide-ranging effects; for example, affecting the way the body moves, control of writing/drawing tools and speech and eye movements. Alongside it, we often see language and mathematical difficulties.

Frequent absences from school (due to ill health) and allergic conditions such as asthma, eczema are common amongst those who have Specific Learning Difficulties. Stress caused by trying to cope with learning difficulties can also cause the child to have more illness than is the norm. This can cause teaching staff to believe that the reason why a child's standard of work has fallen behind his apparent level of ability is because he has not attended school enough, rather than being due to the presence of conditions within the SpLD Profile.

Teaching staff may have little, or no, knowledge of some of the SpLD Profile conditions, and so be unable to recognise them. When SpLDs are present, the child's stress and anxiety may be very apparent. The parent believes that the cause of this anxiety and stress is that her child has a learning difficulty preventing him from reaching his potential. However, the teacher may see the cause as being 'an over-anxious' and pressurising mum who is making the child anxious through an incorrect understanding of the child's ability.

➠ **Graphomotor Dyspraxia**; this is a sub-group of Dyspraxia which affects hand control and the amount of pressure that is used to complete a task. It can show as difficulties in writing and in controlling equipment such as test tubes in science lessons.

➠ **Dyscalculia**, where there can be difficulties in the understanding of numerical information and mathematical concepts/language. (For further details see *Mathematics Solutions – An Introduction to Dyscalculia Parts A and B* by Jan Poustie published by Next Generation.)

➠ **Specific Language Impairment, Central Auditory Processing Disorder (CAPD), Autistic Spectrum Disorder, Asperger's Syndrome, Tourettes Syndrome,** few teachers have the necessary training to recognise these conditions and hardly any even know that CAPD exists.

As a result of conditions such as those mentioned above, the child shows signs of apprehension, insecurity, pessimism, anxiety and stress. The child may become anxious because he feels that he is failing, because he does not find it easy to follow instructions, or because his mind feels so confused and muddled. Some children and adults even wonder whether they are going mad). Gerald Hales' research (see *Dyslexia Matters,* ISBN 1897635117) has found that girls aged 8 to 12 years of above average intelligence (e.g. IQ 115 and above) are particularly prone to being apprehensive and insecure. His research also shows that SpLD children also have a pessimistic patch between the ages of 8 to 12 years, with girls being more affected by this than boys.

The result of hidden Specific Learning Difficulties can be horrendous for the child, the parents and the teachers. All of these have beliefs that are in conflict with each other but all firmly believe that they know the truth.

The parent may well have been concerned for some time that her child has difficulties but has only just told the school of her concerns. She expects immediate action; not to be told 'We will observe the situation this term to see if we can see any difficulties.' If, after several meetings, appropriate provision is still not being offered or difficulties are still not being recognised, she may well become an 'anxious parent'. This will not only affect the relationship between parent and teacher but may spill over to affect the teacher/student relationship and relationships within the family itself. This can result in the parent who raised the concern being without support from either friends or family.

The teacher can feel that the parent is being unreasonable in expecting special treatment for a child that does not need it. As the situation progresses, the relationship between parent and teacher worsens until the trust, which is essential for progress to be made, no longer exists.

The child is the 'piggy in the middle'. Children are aware when they do not fit in. They are aware when they are different, they do not have to be told. Those with Dyspraxia/DCD may frequently knock things flying; those with literacy difficulties are aware that their friends can read and spell with greater ease than they can. The child with Near-vision Dysfunctioning is aware that he often feels sick, has headaches and feels exhausted by the end of the day, while his friends do not. The child with language difficulties/CAPD is aware that he easily misunderstands instructions and feels foolish when he gets them wrong. The child with mathematical difficulties feels stupid when he gets low marks in the times table test, while the child with behavioral difficulties may feel at war with himself.

The lack of recognition of the difficulty, and therefore the lack of provision, is caused by all the parties seeing the situation from vastly different viewpoints based upon their own experience and knowledge.
It is like the story of 'The Six Blind Men and the Elephant'. Each man felt a different part of the elephant and so described it as a completely different beast; e.g. the one who touched the tail described it like a rope.

The teacher sees the tail – that is the anxiety. Every time there is a dispute between the parent and teacher over provision, the tail is twisted. When the child is expected to cope with tasks made difficult by his SpLD, he becomes stressed and anxious, goes home exhausted at the end of the school day, and thus the tail is twisted again. He may be bullied because of his learning difficulties or become depressed because of his lack of success. In severe cases he may be wracked by stomach pains, headaches and feelings of nausea from the moment he wakes until the moment he goes to sleep. Eventually, even the Easter and Christmas holidays do not provide enough time away from school to allow the child to recover. The parent, seeing this, becomes stressed, parental anxiety sets in; she talks with the teacher, who perceives her as an 'anxious parent', and the tail is twisted again.

The parent sees the tusks. If she herself has Specific Learning Difficulties, she knows the problems they cause throughout life and the effect they can have on career choices. If adequate provision is

The road to gaining provision for the student can be very stressful and  sometimes confusing for both parent and professional. If the parents suspect that there is a language difficulty, they could make a direct parental referral to their local Speech and Language unit at their local NHS hospital. If movement difficulties are suspected, then the parents will have to make a direct referral to their local paediatric physiotherapist and paediatric occupational therapist. These are all based at local NHS Trust hospitals and referrals are made via the child's GP.

not swiftly made she feels that she is fighting for her child's rights. She can see the difficulty but does not wish to upset the 'apple cart' too much by frequently drawing the teacher's attention to the child's difficulties, for fear of creating a poor relationship with the teacher. The parent is also trying to keep a balance between these concerns whilst trying to enable her child, and her family, to cope with the emotional and social effects that the difficulties cause. As there is an inheritance factor in each of the SpLD Profile conditions (for example, Dyslexia is eighty per cent inherited) she may also be trying to cope with more than one child's difficulties and possibly her own (or her partner's) difficulties too.

The child is the body of the elephant. He is being pulled in two directions by the tail and the tusks. He may be aware of the parent's concern, especially if provision is not granted quickly (it can take several years to obtain provision). He may be embarrassed, not only by his difficulties but also by the fact that the parent is mentioning them to the teacher, as he may not wish his peers to know that he has problems. He may fear that anything that the teacher does to help may make him more noticeable within the classroom. If he is aware that his parent has concerns, he may also be worried that his difficulties are causing her problems. He may then not tell his parent the problems that are occurring at school. He may be trying to please everyone. In school, he will do whatever he needs to do to cope, so any of the following may happen: work is unfinished; he completes written tasks by writing the minimum amount (and only uses the words he can spell); he pushes himself to the limit and as a consequence feels ill. He may misbehave/daydream or become the 'class clown' to remove himself from an impossible situation; or remove himself completely by truanting from school.

How can this situation be improved?
Imagine that you are in a chemistry lesson. The instructor has asked you to conduct an experiment. You are given the equipment and you attempt to achieve the expected result. If you do not get the right result first time then the instructor will give you tips on how to perfect your experiment. However, if by the end of the lesson you still do not have the expected result he will ask you to take it 'on trust' that he is right on the basis of past research. He will explain to you that you did not have the right environment (heat, proportions of chemicals etc.) to enable you to gain the correct result using your equipment.

When a parent expresses concern, she, like the chemistry instructor, gives tips to her child's teacher on how to recognise the child's problems (including reports from other professionals). Her child's teacher, like the student conducting the experiment, may not reach the same conclusion, because he does not have the correct environment (i.e. knowledge and experience). The teacher cannot see the learning difficulties and so will make no provision for them. He is unable to make the leap of faith that the student chemist has to make, and accept 'on trust' the external specialist's advice.

The SENCO/AENCO becomes involved

At this point, some parents may be lucky. Either the class teacher or the parent discusses the child with the SENCO. The SENCO may accept that difficulties are present and refer the child to the school's LEA liaison professional (e.g. EP/SENST) who makes a positive assessment. If the problems are severe then he will be referred for a Statement of Special Education Needs, where all or part of his provision may be LEA funded unless the LEA has already devolved (given) its funds to the school. If his problems are less severe, he will be placed on School Action (SA) or School Action Plus (SAP), as defined in COP 2002, with the provision coming out of the school budget. (For COP 1994 stages, see page vi.) In 2002 LEAs will be required to publish details of the support arrangements that schools should supply from within their own budgets for students on SA and SAP.[1] If all goes well, appropriate and adequate provision will occur, resulting in:

➼   A working partnership being established between all parties.

➼   An Individual Education Plan (IEP) being drawn up which states the SEN provision that the child will receive.

➼   Harmony existing between the parties.

➼   The child being enabled to succeed, such that everyone, to a greater or lesser degree, is happy.

However, the above situation may not occur. Instead three different situations can emerge, in the first of which conflict is avoided, whereas it is almost inevitable in the others.

1.   The parent may say that she is worried about the child's progress/learning ability etc. If the SENCO/class teacher cannot see a cause for concern, then both he and the parent should continue to observe the child until they are both content that no special needs are present. *(In the past, the SENCO would have entered the child's name on to the Special Educational Needs Register as defined by Stage 1 of the COP 1994. The child's name stayed on the register until both the school and the parent agreed that the child had no special needs. It is thought that many SENCOs will continue with the practice of holding an SEN register, even though this register is not mentioned in the new COP 2002.)*

Glossary of terms
For ease of use the term SENCO is used in this book. Definitions of SENCO/AENCO, EPs, SENST and severe SpLD can be found in the Glossary section of Appendix 3 (page 39-40).

Early Education Settings
These consist of any educational establishment that receive government funding to provide early education for children aged 3 – 5 years (see COP 2002 para. 4:5). SEN children in such establishments may be placed at Early Years Action or Early Years Action Plus. These stages correspond to the similarly named stages used when the child is of compulsory school age. There is actually an overlap between Early Years and School stages as most children start school at age five years (with some attending as a 'rising – five'; e.g. when only four years old.)

IEPs
IEPs should be used when students are at Early Years/School Action or Action Plus or if the student has a Statement. IEPs are explained in detail in Section 5 of the SEN Toolkit which accompanies the COP 2002.

All our SpLD children should be the recipients of educational 'good practice', but with a verbal agreement rather than a written IEP this cannot be guaranteed. What may be overlooked is that a verbal agreement, with its attendant ambiguity, and lack of fixed goalposts, is likely to increase the tension between parties. Thus a verbal IEP will worsen the conflict that may already be present between them. This situation could be avoided if all schools always put a child's SpLD provision into a written format so that all parties know where they stand. However, the increasing number of IEPs in schools is making the writing and reviewing of them such a time-consuming job for SENCOs that many feel they are gradually being submerged under a paper mountain. Computer programs can help generate IEPs. Section 5 of the SEN Toolkit (paras 20 and 21) refers to the delegation of the designing and delivery of IEPs to class and subject teachers. This still leaves the problem of staff reading and taking note of the IEPs. This can be a particular problem in secondary schools, due to the number of staff involved.

2. No written IEP is drawn up; instead the teacher verbally agrees to provide for the student. The COP only provides guidance; so schools may choose not to adopt all of its procedures. In such cases, however, they will be expected to achieve the same ends by different means. This may result in some parents having to rely upon a verbal agreement rather than a written IEP as detailed in the COP 2002.[2] Few people would agree to a verbal contract without having anything in writing to define specification of the goods bought and the date of delivery. Some teachers, however, may prefer a verbal agreement. They feel that an IEP with its defined targets and the necessary negotiation between parent, child and school (as to what the targets are, how they are to be achieved, the expected result and the time frame by which they will be evaluated) will be difficult to agree.

3. The parent may feel that the provision in the IEP (written or oral) is inadequate even after negotiation with the SENCO, or that the student's SpLDs are not recognised by the SENCO.

The result when either number 2 or 3 above occurs is that the parent has to carry on alone along the stony road to provision. (Alternatively, the teacher may know that there is a problem but be unable to persuade the parent to agree to an assessment or make the necessary referral to her GP; e.g. for an assessment for Dyspraxia/DCD. This results in both the teacher and the student becoming very frustrated with their situation.)

The road to gaining provision can be very stony and very isolating for the parent, and stressful for the child, parent and school.

Besides the parent providing 'tips' to the teacher on the child's special needs (like the chemistry instructor in the example mentioned earlier), the government also provides tips on how to meet the needs of special needs children. This can be seen in the guidance within the COP 2002 and the SEN Toolkit which accompanies it (see Appendix 3). All too often, when the child's SpLDs are hidden, neither of these systems work effectively, which results in the child's needs not being met and the relationship between the parent and the teacher becomes strained. The following options may then need to be considered.

Approaching a local support group

By now the parent will hopefully have approached the appropriate local support groups. The relevant national group (e.g. the British Dyslexia Association, the Dyspraxia Foundation) would have provided her with contact details for the group nearest to her (see

Appendix 2). She may take advice from these organisations regarding gaining an assessment of her child's intelligence and/or confirmation of the child's learning difficulties. The support provided by these organisations enables the parent to cope with an increasingly stressful situation. Many professionals do not realise that they too can receive help and support from these agencies.

Private specialist tuition
The parent may, by now, be so concerned that she arranges for her child to receive specialist lessons after school from a suitably qualified private tutor to help the child overcome the main areas of difficulty. The parent is now in a 'catch-22' situation. All specialists in the SpLD field agree that the earlier the child receives correct intervention the less his/her SpLDs will affect him/her in later life. By providing such early intervention, the parent will be reducing the social, academic and emotional affects of SpLD, but the non-specialist class teacher may have even less chance of being able to see the child's difficulties within the classroom. The family is also now under greater pressure, since they have to fund the cost of extra lessons. The parent may be very concerned about the child but may have only minimal (or no) support from her partner/friends/relatives, or indeed the school. This combination of anxiety, lack of support and reduced family finances may result in the break-up of the family unit. This may result in the teacher believing that emotional problems to do with the home are causing the child's difficulties.

Direct parental referrals to LEA/medical professionals
By making such referrals (which often result in a much earlier assessment date) a parent can gain some free assessments of her child. (Some LEAs allow direct parental referral to their Psychological Service/SENST). She would need to insist on a full assessment of the child, as otherwise her suspicions might not be confirmed - a full assessment takes about one and half hours or more. Usually EPs have access to comprehensive forms of IQ assessment (e.g. WISC and BAS) but, in some LEAs, SENST professionals conduct such assessments under supervision of EPs.

The parent may decide to pay privately for an assessment of her child; e.g. via an Educational Psychologist, specialist school or AMBDA professional and/or medical assessment. Prices for such assessments vary tremendously, with some educational assessments costing as little as £200 whilst some medical/ educational assessments cost £800+. If the parent suspects that the learning difficulties relate in part to a visual problem, then she may also choose to have a behavioural optometrist assessment (tel. 01277 624916 for contact details). However,

The parent may become so concerned that she has the child assessed by various private specialists who are able to diagnose Specific Learning Difficulties. These provide her with reports on the child, proving the presence of SpLD, and make recommendations to help the child overcome his problems. Unfortunately, schools may decide to ignore reports from such private specialists, and, even if the LEA agrees with the reports, the school may continue not to provide for the student's specific learning difficulties. It is very unwise for a school to ignore a request for an assessment made by another professional; e.g. a GP. Such actions can result in a Court of Law declaring the school to be in breach of contract or negligent (see pages xi and 42).

AMBDA = Associate Member of the British Dyslexia Association

Training is likely to be needed for our educators so that they can enable our SpLD students to be able contribute effectively their views of their provision. The importance of enabling such students to contribute to the discussion on their provision (and strategies for doing so) are discussed in Section 3 of the COP 2002. An essential part of this process is the student understanding the conditions that are present. Here a label (though much frowned upon by many professionals) may be essential; e.g. it is far better to think of oneself as having Dyslexia than to believe that one is 'thick' or 'mad'. The latter is the belief held by some ADHD students until their condition is explained to them. Necessary techniques for enabling SpLD students to express their views include the use of 'open questions'; e.g. 'How do you think you learn best?' (Also see Section 4 of the SEN Toolkit which accompanies the COP 2002.)

the school may not accept the findings of these reports if they still cannot see evidence in the classroom that the difficulties exist and so provision may still not be made. Note: parents should only provide copies (not the originals) of reports to the school. Conflict can arise if the school loses a report and then (since they do not have the report) claims that there is no reason to provide the desired provision.

The OFSTED inspection
If the school is due for an OFSTED inspection the parent may voice her concerns at the parent's meeting held by the OFSTED inspectors prior to the inspection of the school. She may also mention her concerns via a confidential questionnaire, and provide the inspectors with written documentation of the difficulty she is having in gaining provision for her child. As a result, she may find that the OFSTED report on the school includes a general reference to her problem under the 'Parents' and carers' views of the school' section. If the problem is great enough, then she will also find mention of it in the 'What should the school do to improve further?' section, which is found at the end of the report. How the school intends to achieve these improvements has to be written into the school's Action Plan which must be prepared within forty working days after receiving the full report (excluding Easter, Christmas and Summer Holidays). Generally speaking, it is the parents and governors who have to ensure that the Action Plan, is implemented, as OFSTED was not established to follow-up every school Action Plan. Schools that are in Special Measures (i.e. failing or likely to fail), or that have serious and significant weaknesses are automatically followed up. Outside of these groups, only a limited number of Action Plans are followed up. (See Appendix 3, page 41 for further details on OFSTED.)

Use the Disagreement Resolution Service (DRS)
This is very much new territory, for no-one knows how it will work out, this being a new service introduced by the COP 2002 (which lays down minimum standards for it). Although this service has to be provided by the LEA, it is expected to be both independent of it and informal.[3] The parent's legal right to appeal to the SEN Tribunal is not affected by using the DRS, which can be used whilst an appeal is being made. Use of the DRS may reduce or resolve the conflict, open the doors to better communication and the child may then receive the provision that he requires. However, although the theory behind the service is a good one, no-one knows how effective it will be in practice.

Where is the child in this process?
In the past, the child may have had very little say in the matter, whether or not he has received provision. The COP 2002 devotes

the whole of its Section 3 to Pupil Participation[4], including explaining how teachers need to train children in developing the skills needed to explain their views.[5] A new source of conflict may arise here, for some adults (the teachers, parents or both) may feel reluctant to overly involve the child, believing that 'adults know best'. This situation is a little like taking a horse to water and not being able to make him drink! If the horse (the student) has some choice as to what happens (and when) then he is more likely to 'drink' (take an active part in/benefit from the provision). Conflict may also arise because one set of adults (professionals or parents) will be listening to the child whilst the other will be paying lip-service to the student's views. The fact that educators have not taken due consideration of the student's views in the past is reflected in the fact that the COP 2002 draws educationalist's attention to the need for mutual respect when dealing with SEN children.[6] It also mentions that children have the right to express opinions and have their views taken into consideration, under The *United Nations Convention on the Rights of the Child*[7]. COP 2002 recommends the use of a Pupil Report Form[8] for recording the views of the student when a Statutory Assessment of the student's Special Educational Needs (which can lead to a Statement) is being made. A similar document is needed when parents/professionals first raise concerns as to whether the student has special needs. The photocopiable *Pupil Report Forms* in Book I of this library can be used for both purposes. Suggestions for consulting children and young people can also be found in the SEN Toolkit which accompanies COP 2002 (see page vi for details on how to obtain the COP 2002).

Exceptional intellectual ability and SpLD
(See page 37 for details of the National Association for Gifted Children.)

Each of the two commonly used IQ tests in Britain use different terms to describe the exceptional intellectual ability of the 2% of the child population who have an IQ of 130 and above. (WISC III UK uses the term 'exceptionally high' whilst BAS II uses the term 'very high'.) LEAs may describe these children as being Gifted and Talented. Usually the LEA has a special advisor for such children. Problems in being able to recognise learning difficulties can be worsened if the child has exceptional intellectual ability, SpLDs and is of primary school age. This is because few children come into this category and therefore primary-school teachers especially (due to the small size of their schools) are unlikely to meet them very often. How can teachers recognise what they have never seen before? Such individuals are often only spotted in late secondary school or adulthood. The

'It is thought that around 5 – 10% of gifted children (that is, somewhere between 1 in 200 and 1 in 400 children) could also have a learning disability; this can include sensory impairment, physical disability or specific learning difficulty'

(Louise Porter, *Gifted Young Children*, page 235, pub. OUP, 1999. The source for her information is: Dix, J. and Schafer, S. 1996, 'From paradox to performance: practical strategies for identifying and teaching' GT/LD students, in *Gifted Child Today*, vol. 19, no. 1, pp. 22–4 and 28–9.) Note: in the above figures the 'gifted' category is regarded as being 5% of the population.

Gifted children and learning difficulties

Louise Porter states that: 'approximately 2%–5% of children with disabilities may also be gifted'. (*Gifted Young Children*, pp. 235–6. Her sources of information were:

Johnson, L. J., Karnes M. B., and Carrr, V. W. 1997, 'Providing services to children with gifts and disabilities : a critical need' in *Handbook of Gifted Education* (2nd edn), Boston, MA.

Whitmore J. R. (1981), 'Gifted children with handicapping conditions: a new frontier' in *Exceptional Children*, vol. 48 no. 2, pp. 106–14.

Yewchuk C. R. & Lupart J. L., (1993) 'Gifted handicapped: a desultory duality' in *International Handbook of Research and Development of Giftedness and Talent*, K. A. Heller, F. J. Monks and A. H. Passow, (eds), Pergamon Press, Oxford.

chartered educational psychologist Dr. Peter Gardner states:

> Though research studies and experts differ in their attributions of the incidence of severity, there does appear to be agreement that approximately one child in twenty-five shows evidence of severe Specific Learning Difficulties and one child in six shows evidence of milder difficulties which are still causing problems in the classroom.

If teachers accept the diagnosis of SpLD but see that the child is performing at chronological age, they may feel that the child has no greater problem in learning than other children[9], and they may therefore conclude that no intervention is needed. However, as Dr Peter Gardner says:

> All teachers consider it their duty to maximise the potential of each child. It is unlikely that a teacher would expect a pupil of more limited potential to achieve their chronological age level. Therefore, it should also be the case that (all things being equal) the teacher should expect the very intellectually able pupil to attain a level above his chronological age appropriate to his intellect.

Gardner's comments are especially apt in the light of the fact that paragraph 1:1 of the COP 2002 mentions that its guidance is aimed at SEN students reaching their full potential.[10] If neither the giftedness nor the SpLDs of the student are recognised, then both child and parents can be on a very slippery slope indeed.

The parent's concerns increase

The child's behaviour may deteriorate; he may become aggressive and demanding, have stomach aches/headaches and feel sick. He may have poor sleeping habits, with difficulties going to sleep and frequent waking during the night. Now both child and parent feel permanently tired. The child may be receiving private intervention but various factors may be causing him stress during the school day; for example, the amount of copying, writing and reading that he has to do without the use of a spellchecker or computer. (Many schools have so few computers that there is no way that the child could do most of his work on a computer unless the parent provides it, or unless one is provided via a Local Educational Authority Statement.)

Communication between educational professionals and the parents may break down

The parent may receive little or no support from the school. This can happen even after the parent has discussed the issues with the school governors. (The governors may support a school's actions on the basis that the teachers are unable to see difficulties and therefore unable to respond to them.) The COP 2002 draws the professional's attention to the pressure that the parent is under and outlines key principles in communicating and working in partnership with parents as being:

➼ positive attitudes to parents,

➼ the provision of user-friendly information. [11]

The school can feel harassed

By this stage, the school may well feel that they are being harassed by a parent who has unreasonable expectations of both her child and the school. The school and parent are now in conflict and communication may become difficult for both of them. The parent, realising this, may ask for intervention by The Parent Partnership Officer (PPO) see Section 2 of the SEN Toolkit which accompanies the COP 2002. The PPO's name and telephone number is available from the LEA. The PPO may be able to re-establish the lines of communication between the parent and the school, and also may be able to help both parties negotiate a better situation, but he or she has no power over what the school does.

Involving the Local Education Authority (LEA)

Eventually the parent (if she lives within a LEA that allows this) may involve the Authority by making a direct parental referral to the IEA's Special Educational Needs Department. If it accepts the findings of the specialists, it will make recommendations to the school, which include detailing what the difficulties are and the areas in which provision needs to be made. However, the school may refuse to accept the recommendations of its LEA, as it is unable to see evidence of any Specific Learning Difficulties within the classroom. Alternatively, the school may feel that the child should not be prioritised for provision as they have students who are 'far worse than he is'.

By this stage no one is happy

The parent, the child and the rest of the family are under great stress, as may be the school too. There is no easy solution, because both parents and the school each still believe that they are correct. The parent and child now have several choices, they can:

1. Change to another LEA school (and hope that they will have better luck next time). The child will have to cope with making new friends, learn to trust that the teacher/teaching assistant will meet his needs and cope with the changes in school routine - adjustments that many SpLD children find daunting. The parent may have little trust in teachers by now and may fear that her child will still not receive the provision he needs.

2. Move the child to a private school specialising in Specific Learning Difficulties. This, though, may cost a great deal of money and the strain of funding it will affect the whole family.

If the teacher is still unable to see the child's learning difficulties, they do not exist in his view and therefore no provision is made. The school and parent are now in conflict, and communication may become very difficult for both parties. The teacher may feel that he is failing the child, and therefore the family. In the past, teachers have seen themselves as 'informers' – 'Your child has this difficulty; we will do this about it.' They may feel that because of their experience and qualifications 'they know best'. Now they are expected to discuss provision.

Negotiation requires compromise and agreement between the parties. It requires skills that have not been part of the teacher's training. He may feel out of his depth. He may continue to only use his 'informing skills', which to the parent may seem autocratic and part of a 'them and us' situation.

Education Otherwise
PO Box 7420, London N99 SG.
Emergency helpline: 08700 7300074
Website:
http://www.education-otherwise.org
E-mail:
enquiries@education-otherwise.org
This is an umbrella organisation for families who are teaching their children at home. It provides self-help, support and information. For information, send an A5 stamped addressed envelope.

The best of these specialist schools have a 'whole school' policy. Here every teacher is aware of the difficulties that SpLDs cause in every subject – though not every teacher may have an appropriate qualification in the teaching of those with Specific Learning Difficulties. (A list of Specialist Schools is obtainable from CReSTeD, Tel/.Fax. 01242 604852, www.crested.org.uk)

3. Take the child out of the education system and teach him at home. This can itself cause difficulties; for example, it may mean that the family will be deprived of the mother's income and that the student may have difficulty finding other children during the school day with whom to relate. (Note: it is legal to teach your child at home even if you are not a qualified teacher.)

4. Make a request for a Statutory Assessment under section 329 of the 1996 Education Act. Some people may find that section 328 applies instead (see Part IV, Chapter 1 of the Act at: www.hmso.gov.uk/acts/acts1996/1996056.htm). Such a request can be made even if the child attends a private school[12] or is educated at home.[13] The parent may need to take advice from a support group, such as her local Dyslexia Association befriender, to ensure that she makes the request correctly. The LEA only has to comply with this request if they believe that the child probably has special educational needs, and that it is likely that the LEA will need to determine the provision.[14] Generally, the LEA will expect the school to have done everything it can to meet the child's needs before deciding to determine the provision. However, the COP recognises that there will be times when the parent is dissatisfied with school-based provision and then turns to the LEA.[15] When the LEA has completed a statutory assessment, it may issue a Statement of the child's needs.

Appealing to the SEN Tribunal
The LEA can refuse to make the assessment. (An assessment is expensive – it can cost over £2000 to make a full multi-disciplinary assessment, so this may well make an LEA reluctant to assess a child who they feel does not require a Statement). A school cannot appeal to the tribunal. An appeal can only be made by the parents. The tribunal will ask for a copy of the parent's letter in which the request for assessment was made. Very useful letter templates for all the stages of asking for a Statement and appealing against LEA decisions can be found at the IPSEA website: www.ipsea.org.uk Also see www.sentribunal.gov.uk

Once an assessment is made, the LEA can then refuse to

issue a Statement on the grounds that the child's learning difficulties are not severe enough to warrant one. If the LEA refuses either to assess the child or to provide a Statement, then an appeal to reverse the decision can be made to the tribunal.

5. Make a formal complaint to the Secretary of State for education under Section 497 of the 1996 Education Act, in that the governing body of the school has acted unreasonably and unlawfully. (The parent will need to take advice from her local support group (e.g. local Dyslexia Association) on the correct wording of the complaint.)

How is the teacher feeling at this point? He may:

➡ Feel that he is failing the child, and therefore the family, because he cannot get the parent to recognise that the school is correct in its view that the child is having no difficulties with school work and therefore no provision needs to be made.

➡ Feel that he is dealing with a parent who will never be satisfied with anything that he does or says. He therefore can become distressed by the fact that the parent will not stop making demands of him that he feels unable to meet.

➡ Dread every conversation and meeting with the parent. Every statement made by the parent may be analysed to see if the parent is 'having a go' at him.

➡ Feel that he is at risk of losing control of the situation, so be even less ready to discuss the child's learning difficulties with the parent.

➡ Resent the amount of time and energy that this parent is taking when he has children in the school who he feels have far greater needs than this child.

➡ Feel that the parent is being pushy and unreasonable, and that she has unrealistic expectations of the child (and the school) since no child can be good at everything.

The Code of Practice

A parent who understands the COP 2002 will know that it is not being implemented correctly or its guidance followed. He will resent that this is the case and will become anxious regarding the school's knowledge base. The teacher can then feel that he is being bludgeoned with the COP 2002 by the parent and yet another area of conflict has arisen. By now the teacher may have placed the child on one of the stages of the COP 2002 (e.g. School Action or School Action Plus) but the parent may feel that more intervention is required. Some

Under the Special Educational Needs and Disability Act 2001 an appeal against the LEAs decision not to assess or not to award a Statement can be made to the SEN Tribunal no matter whether they or the school made the original request for the statutory assessment/Statement.

For further information about how parents can make a complaint about their child's provision see complaints section in Appendix 3, page 40.

The teacher may feel intimidated by the parent's knowledge of Specific Learning Difficulties. Like a doctor who resents the patient telling him the diagnosis, the teacher may feel that his experience and hard-earned qualifications are regarded as worthless or imperfect.

The teacher may feel intimidated by the Code of Practice. (All schools by law must take notice of what the COP says and are not permitted to ignore it.[16]. This fact alone can make a teacher feel insecure. See Appendix 3 Implementation of the COP 2002 on page 40.

teachers still do not realise that children do not have to progress through all the stages. If the parent knows the COP 2002, this again will be an area for conflict. In other cases, the teacher is trying to do his best with limited resources and may not wish to put the child at a higher stage of the COP 2002, which will involve more funding. The parent regards the provision as inadequate, insufficient or inappropriate whilst the teacher wonders if this parent will ever be satisfied with the provision that the school makes. The teacher may feel that:

▸▸ his knowledge base is being slighted, especially if he has a specialist qualification in Special Needs. He may be unaware that a single module dedicated to SpLD in a Special Needs course is unlikely to have given him the ability to access, recognise and provide for the child with hidden complex SpLD difficulties;

▸▸ he is vulnerable, that he is being personally criticised by the parent and that his work in the classroom is not appreciated;

▸▸ if he recognises that the child has learning difficulties then the parent will become more demanding. He may fear that other parents will similarly start to expect more for their children, and that there is no way his limited resources can cope with this;

▸▸ on the defensive all the time, and feel that the problem is not with the school but with the parent. Consequently, he will look for events at home that are making the child anxious and put the child/parent relationship under severe scrutiny.

By now, he may feel very distressed, isolated and vulnerable especially if the parent tries to travel further along the road of gaining provision by asking the LEA for a Statement or by making a formal complaint to the Secretary of State for Education on the grounds that the school is acting unlawfully and unreasonably. The school can then be in crisis: it lacks the knowledge to move forward yet feels that it cannot go back on what it has said in the past, since that would compromise its position. A dislike for the parent, who the teaching staff feel is causing the crisis in the first place, can then become apparent.

The need for partnership between schools and parents

In the past, many parents have had their concerns regarding their children ignored or felt intimidated when raising their concerns. The government recognises that in far too many cases schools have not worked in partnership with parents. Thus, the

COP 2002 emphasises the need for parent/professional partnership if success is to be achieved.[17] The government is so aware of the importance of this partnership that Section 2 of the COP 2002 is devoted to it[18] and even makes reference to schools using the expertise of parents. (Parents have often accessed a great deal of knowledge regarding the condition/s which cause their child's difficulties). However, the teacher may already feel that the parent is trying to usurp his position and authority. He may dread the appearance of the parent at the classroom door and feel threatened by the parent's knowledge base. It may therefore be very difficult for him to accept and follow these guidelines.

By now the teacher may well be as frustrated as the parent and the child

The parent and the reports say that the difficulties exist and are causing problems for the child at school. At this point, the teacher may decide that the SpLDs exist. Since he cannot see any evidence of them in the classroom, he believes that they cannot be causing the child any difficulties and therefore no provision is necessary.

A very different picture can emerge here, for there could also be conflict between educational professionals regarding the child's provision within the school

The school's liaison Educational Psychologist (EP) may disagree with the SENCO or vice versa (see page 24). A situation can arise where both the SENCO and the parent accept the presence of the specific learning difficulties (and their effect on learning/behaviour) and unite to fight for the student's provision. As one SENCO says:

> I've not had a liaison EP initiate an assessment for some seven or eight years. I've had to advise parents about their right to request formal assessment and dutifully submitted the necessary paperwork. I've also successfully appeared as 'expert witness' in support of parents 'against' the LEA at Tribunal.

However, parents are only likely to get this sort of support if the SENCO is very well-informed about SpLD, is very dedicated to his students and is prepared (and able) to give a great deal of free time to support them.

The COP 1994 (para. 2:15) stated with reference to the SENCO that 'in a small school, one person may take on this role, possibly the head or deputy'. The result of this is that the SENCO (especially in a primary school) may not necessarily be

Several of the parties involved with the student may disagree with each other on how to best provide for the student. For example, an EP (private or LEA-based) may come to a conclusion and produce proposals which are not accepted by the other professionals (e.g. the school). Alternatively, a medical professional may conclude that a student requires assessment/provision; for example, for ADHD/ADD, but the school may not put the same high priority on the particular student's needs. Thus a 'will not listen/will not take notice' situation can arise between any of the parties.

the teacher with the most experience or interest in SpLD. Alternatively, the SENCO may know a great deal about the general field of Special Needs but know little about SpLD (or may know little about either and still be in the process of learning about them). Thus the very difficult situation can arise where a class teacher, supply teacher or teaching assistant (TA), recognises the learning difficulties but the SENCO/Headteacher does not. A part-time teacher, supply teacher or TA may be wary of 'rocking the boat' for fear of losing his/her teaching/ classroom support hours. The full-time teacher is only too aware as to who will be writing his next reference. In such cases, the teacher/TA may well be very limited in what he can do without upsetting the SENCO and the Headteacher.

Teaching Assistants (Learning Support Assistants)
Teaching assistants (Specialist Teaching Assistants in particular) are most probably one of the most underpaid and unappreciated educators in the UK's educational system, yet in many of our schools they provide the bulk of SEN provision. Their SENCOs know how valuable they are to the work of the school yet the pay is so appalling that those who are single may be in a 'poverty trap'. The fact that our education system treats so many of these invaluable members of staff so poorly is an indication of the way in which special needs is really regarded by this country. We seem to lack a coherence across the UK as to how TAs are employed, with some having permanent contracts, and some temporary ones. TAs who provide SEN students with one-to-one support may find themselves not getting paid when the student is off sick. (Increased absences are typical of students with special needs so this can markedly reduce the TA's pay). Those supporting Year-11 students may find that their pay is stopped as soon as their students go on study leave and that they are not paid both for the end of the summer term and for the summer holiday. Organisations that provide training and permanent contracts for their TAs find that they are able to retain experienced and knowledgeable staff, who can then provide better provision for their students. TA's responsibilities have steadily increased over the last decade without a corresponding increase in pay. If our government really values them, it would ensure that TAs have a career structure, be adequately trained, be permanent members of staff throughout the UK and be paid during holidays.

The teacher/TA may be limited to emotionally supporting the child and making minor adjustments to the way in which he is taught
One of the most useful things a teacher can do is to boost the

As a result of the inability to assess, recognise and provide for the child to the satisfaction of the parent, coupled with his awareness of the school's limited resources, a teacher may decide to opt out. He may feel that the parent will never be content, so there is no point in trying. The result is that he offers no provision at all and only communicates with the parent about the child's possible special needs when the parent insists upon a discussion.

child's confidence by finding an area in which he has more than average skill, and then enable him to demonstrate his talents within the classroom. The teacher/TA is forever in a balancing act between the 'devil and the deep blue sea' as he also has to have regular dealings with the parent whilst knowing that correct provision is not being made.

The parent who has travelled along the stony road of trying to gain provision may well be exhausted by now

Non-provision effects on the family

The attempt to gain provision may have caused serious rifts within the family. Brothers and sisters may become jealous of the child who gets away with aggression, climbs into mum and dad's bed and generally seems to receive more attention than they do. Sometimes a divorce is the result of one of the parents no longer being able to cope with the stress caused by the non-provision. In some, though thankfully few, cases the child takes the tragic step of opting out by committing suicide.

Parental stress and dissatisfaction

The parent may decide to give up trying for provision because the stress (and work involved) is too much. She and the child may try to make the best of a very bad situation, with the parent remaining dissatisfied with the child's education throughout the child's school life.

The price of non-provision

The child only fulfills his potential if he is lucky and meets a teacher that teaches him in the way that he needs if he is to learn. If he is unlucky he will never recover from the emotional aspects of SpLD, such as being bullied and teased by his peers for his difficulties, always feeling a failure, being a 'round peg' in the 'square hole' of his school environment. He may retreat from society as he becomes more and more convinced that society has never helped him. He may then join the large proportion (40%+) of the prison population who have Specific Learning Difficulties. (Even those who are sent to prison as juvenile offenders and who have a Local Education Authority Statement of Educational Need may not receive appropriate or adequate provision. This is because the evidence of their learning difficulties, which was originally produced as a result of an assessment leading to the Statement, often fails to reach the appropriate Prison Education Department. This situation is worsened by the fact that prisoners move from one penal institution to another, with the continual reassessment which that entails.)

Teaching Assistants (TAs)
TAs may be known as Learning Support Assistants (LSAs) in some schools. Some are highly trained but others are not. Indeed some find themselves starting work dealing with a student who has highly complex special needs without any training at all! Most feel that they are provided with far too little SEN/SpLD training. We thus have a situation where, unbeknown to the parents, a student with a Statement may actually not receive specialist provision but instead receive provision via an untrained TA. There are various courses available to TAs; e.g. CLANSA and CACHE. The professional organisation for TAs is: CLASS (contact: M G Stephenson, 83 Maple Road, Dartford, DA1 2QY Tel. 01322 407443).
There is also a website for TAs: www.spare-chair.com

Provision for Specific Learning Difficulties by Jan Poustie   ISBN 1 901544 18 4

Making the whole situation worse may be the fact that the teacher:

➡ may not fully understand the reports that the parent has given to him regarding the child's learning difficulties. He may be unhappy about admitting this either to the parent or to other professionals/teachers for fear of appearing inadequate.

➡ may assume any or all of the following: that the child is lying about his difficulties to his parent; that the child is lazy, careless or has an attitude problem. This occurs because the standard of an SpLD child's work is often inconsistent and so the teacher may observe that the child may be able to do the work sometimes with comparative ease.

Hidden Specific Learning Difficulties can create a 'no-win' situation for all the parties involved

To go back to the original analogy of the Six Blind Men and the Elephant. From the parent's point of view, each meeting, with its associated failure to gain adequate provision, chips away at 'the tusks' until only the stumps are left – the parent has no more fight in her.

The teacher

From the teacher's point of view, each meeting (with its associated failure to get the parent to understand that no provision is necessary or that the present provision is sufficient) twists 'the tail' again. In the end it becomes a mass of knots and tight curls that destroys the teacher/parent relationship.

The child

From the child's point of view, for each week that s/he does not receive adequate provision 'the body' starves until it becomes emaciated and is no longer able to function adequately in its environment.

Non-recognition of the small signs of SpLD

Since the teacher cannot recognise what he cannot see, he is therefore unable to make provision for it. He has not seen those small signs that indicate all is not well with the child's learning processes. The teacher has not seen:

➡ the associated body movements when the child is working at academic tasks;

➡ the fidgeting and hair twisting as the child has to work extra hard to control his body and visual functions, which can indicate Dyspraxia/DCD or Near-vision Dysfunctioning;

➡ nor does he understand the reason for the smile of relief on the child's face as he greets his parent at the end of an exhausting and frustrating school day;

➡ the hooked hand and distorted paper position, which can indicate difficulties with writing and possible Near-vision Dysfunctioning;

➡ the odd sitting position favoured by the child (again, a possible indicator of Dyspraxia/DCD);

➡ that the impulsive child who leaps into tasks, often interrupts and just cannot wait his turn, may well have Attention Deficit Disorder (ADD). How on earth can the daydreamer who has opted out because he has been told once too often not to dominate the classroom discussions also be affected by ADD?!

The signs are so small, yet the underlying difficulty and stress can be so great. The signs are like the mouse rustling through the hedgerow. They are too small to be of any significance in the general landscape, except to the sharp, watchful eye of a parent/specialist teacher, who knows that such signs can lead to the discovery of something much bigger.

The best that parents may be able to achieve is to provide the understanding, support and love that the child needs. When the child asks them 'Why does no one help me? Why don't they understand that I have a problem?' they will need to explain rationally and unemotively why our present educational system is unable to help him. Hopefully this may prevent the child from growing up hating 'the system' and the society that it represents, and eventually electing to become a social outcast .

The parent

She may have had concerns for several years before she even made the school aware of them. Thus, from her initial concern, it may have taken five or six years to reach this stage. Now the parent may feel the need to withdraw both herself and the child from the situation (by electing to educate him at home for a while) so that both can gradually recover from the emotional battering their experience has given them. The parent sees the difficulties but cannot convince the school and thus endures years of frustration, anxiety and stress.

Some parents decide never to try to gain provision via the state system

They realise that it may never be successful and purposefully hide their child's difficulties from the teacher. They pay for private tuition from a specialist tutor to help the child overcome as many of his difficulties as possible. Sometimes these children come to light when they start their GCSE course. (The teacher may realise that the child is struggling or the parents may finally voice their concern fearing that their child's career choices will be limited by poor grades.) Sometimes individuals only find out in adulthood the reason for their struggle at school.

The child

He may never receive the provision that he needs and may well have to adjust to years of frustration and a feeling of inadequacy or failure. Whatever the parent gains for him is likely to be a compromise between what the parent knows he needs and what she can obtain for him. However, although the school may not accept or provide for the child's needs, few parents will be able to ignore that they exist. The child always loses. Both his family and teacher are under stress, and academic work is a struggle. His whole personality may be affected by the intolerable situation he is in. As one parent observed

> He always sang until he started school. I only realised that he had stopped singing throughout the whole of his school life when he started to sing again the day after he completed his A levels.

Our Specific Learning Difficulty children should be able to sing, they should be enabled to be at peace with their world.

Provision for Specific Learning Difficulties by Jan Poustie   ISBN 1 901544 18 4

The SENCO-forum is a UK-based Internet group sponsored by the government, membership of which is recommended for all SENCOs in the COP 2002.[19]
To join, send an e-mail to: majordomo@ngfl.gov.uk
Leave the 'subject line' blank and in the body of the message write: subscribe senco-forum. It is not open to parents. Members include UK state and private school SENCOs, private SpLD tutors, EPs and overseas educators. It is invaluable as a source of support (its like a virtual reality staff room) and it is also an exceptionally quick source of information. Members can ask just about any question and no one will think the less of them even when the question was about something very basic.

The Solution
Meet the needs of the SENCOs

The SENCOs have a public voice in that many are now members of an Internet group called SENCO-forum. Looking through the strands of conversations over the last year it becomes apparent that, as a body, SENCOs have several major concerns, of which a few are:

➠ Inclusion: This relates to the method/resources by which all students (no matter what their disabilities) have their needs met within mainstream schooling. It is felt that this is not properly resourced. It is also felt that it is difficult to marry this ideal with government pressures to increase standards, including the school's position on the school league tables which are published yearly.

➠ Bureaucracy/paperwork etc. We appear to have created a climate in the UK where the government's pressure to produce precise and mountains of paperwork (rather than encouraging and praising creativity and spontaneity) is not only destroying some of our best teachers but is putting an intolerable strain upon SENCOs in particular. The result is that many of our most specialised teachers have less teaching time. (Some schools have already started to employ a new type of TA who is trained to do part of the administrative role of the SENCO. All schools needs such TAs, and these in turn need specialist training for this new role.)

On top of all this, the SENCO role is being made increasingly more difficult because of:

➠ Increased 'testing' of children (e.g. SATs) that put special needs children into public situations where they may repeatedly be seen to 'fail'.

➠ The failure of the Literacy and Numeracy strategies to meet the needs of the least able pupils.

Some SENCOs have an excellent relationship with their LEA/ EPs. Others, however, are increasingly disillusioned with their LEAs and EPs whom they feel are working in some cases to make it as difficult as possible for parents and schools to obtain additional resources to meet children's needs effectively. This is particularly worrying, for how can the government expect to improve the SEN provision for our children if some of our SENCOs do not trust their own LEAs/EPs?

Training the educators

There is hope. A solution is possible for this seemingly impossible situation but it will take time and commitment on the part of our educators. It is recognised, by those working in the SpLD field, that the only way to improve this situation for teacher, parent and child is for all educators (no matter what subject or age group they teach) to have a minimum training in the field of Specific Learning Difficulties. Many educators are aware of their lack of knowledge in this field and are concerned by it, as they wish to do their best for all the children and students in their care. However, they may not know where they can receive training. Details of training for each of the SpLD Profile conditions can be obtained from the relevant charities in Appendix 2. (Parents please note that some of these bodies offer courses that you too can attend.) Schools can also approach their LEA and ask for SpLD in-service training.

Improve the communication skills of educational professionals

For many years, doctors have been trained in appropriate 'bedside manners'. Our educators similarly need training. All teachers should be trained to negotiate with both the other professionals with whom they will have to deal and with the parents. Training will need to include how to deal with distressed parents. Having negotiating skills can make all the difference in preventing a parent/teacher situation spiralling out of control, with loss of trust on both sides. The use of the 'How I feel' sheets in Book 1 of this library may help enable parents and teachers to have a constructive relationship. The COP 2002 recommends that Parent Partnership Officers provide educational staff with training to improve good communication and relationships with parents.[20] Training is also recommended for these staff on how to consult students (and deal with parents) when communication difficulties are present.[21] Those with communication difficulties are at a great disadvantage when trying to explain their problems and for parents this can be incredibly stressful.

Training the governors

The British Dyslexia Association (see Appendix 2) do arrange lectures specifically for school governors. Given the complexity of the legal and financial sides of SEN provision, it is only too easy for governors to be under-informed, and so prefer to leave special needs matters to the staff. The COP 2002 is a very large and complex document, and many governors may therefore shy away from reading it. The fact that governors are not paid for their services but give their time on a voluntary basis does not help this situation. However, as power and, in some LEAs, budgets

We need to train all of our educators

Since our children move on to further education it is not just teachers who need training but lecturers in colleges and universities as well. Of vital importance is the training of those who train our teachers. A module that deals with Specific Learning Difficulties to an adequate depth should be a compulsory part of all teacher-training courses, for, as Violet Brand says

> We need to train teachers in their initial teacher training. They need to be made aware of these specific problems that they will be meeting whatever subject they are teaching, whatever age group.

However, with many teachers gaining the one year PGCE qualification, there is little time for such a module and so. Therefore, for many teachers, the only solution is to make this training compulsory in their first year of teaching.

Training priorities
Research shows that early intervention is the nearest 'cure' for Specific Learning Difficulties. It is therefore essential that all of our primary-school teachers and nursery/childcare workers are trained as quickly as possible to recognise, assess, provide for and support children with SpLD.

also are being increasingly devolved to schools (and therefore to the governors who run them) surely it is time that they were paid for their labour in just the same way as local councillors are.

Availability of trained school's inspectors
Changes in the inspection system mean that OFSTED reports no longer have to have a section devoted to SEN, but all subject inspectors are required to report on the SEN provision within their subject. However, although such inspectors have a basic SEN training via OFSTED, they may only have limited knowledge of SpLD. There is a shortage of Special Educational Needs (SEN) trained inspectors, which OFSTED is trying to rectify via Additional Inspector Secondments and by prioritising the assessment of potential SEN Inspection Team Leaders. Schools are inspected by OFSTED inspectors via a tender system. If a school has indicated in its form 's' that it has a specific SEN unit then it will be ensured that the inspection team will include a member with appropriate SEN experience, but an SEN specialist inspector will not necessarily be included otherwise. It was expected that all inspectors would have received one day's training on Inclusion by the end of 2001.

Conclusion
Now that training is available throughout the country all schools that are committed to meeting the needs of their SpLD children should ensure that they have at least one member of staff who is fully trained in this field. They will also ensure that the knowledge of this specialist teacher is used by all teachers in the school and that their SENCO is SpLD trained. Perhaps the first thing a parent should ask a school is whether this is the case, and if not, why not?

'Does this child have a condition within (or associated with) the Specific Learning Difficulties Profile?' should be the first question teachers ask when a parent raises concerns. Only by training, and learning about these conditions will our educators and inspectors be able to recognise all the different forms of these difficulties. Only then can they enable our children and adult students to receive the support and education that they need and deserve.

CHAPTER 3
Conclusion

Throughout the UK there are islands of excellent practice within seas of inadequacy. It is not that some of our teachers do not want to help our students; it is just that they are exhausted, struggling with increasing behavioural problems amongst their students, overloaded with bureaucracy, and hampered by inadequate SpLD training. On top of this, the field of SpLD just seems to get bigger and bigger. It is thus a lottery as to whether a student receives adequate SpLD provision. This situation can only be changed if all of those involved with the student are enabled to develop a better understanding of the conditions covered in this library. Knowledge can be increased through joining a local support group (see Appendix 2) and by reading specialist books; e.g. the rest of this library and the books listed at the end of each chapter. Various agencies (see Appendix 2) hold excellent national and local conferences and lectures for both professionals and parents/adult students. However, many of the educational professionals who may be interested in attending such events are blocked from accessing them by short-sighted headteachers who do not enable their attendance by refusing to provide funding and supply staff. (This is a major problem in some LEAs where they have devolved their budgets to schools; i.e. the school decides where the money goes not the LEA. We also need schools to allow their staff to implement the strategies that they have been taught on courses.

The future: cause and effect!
Of great long-term importance are the issues of diet and environmental factors (mentioned in Books 1 and 6) that increasingly appear to be affecting the functioning of our students. The UK government is currently introducing policies on behaviour management for students with behavioural difficulties but this strategy presumes that aggressive behaviours etc. are within the student's control. Some readers may know of the theory of Ockham's Razor, which suggests that when there is an obvious answer we should not seek complex solutions. If we apply this simple principle, then we are faced with an unpalatable truth. There is mounting scientific evidence indicating that certain foods and chemicals taken into our bodies through our diet (or missing from our diet) are in fact responsible for at least some of the increasing number of

Many AENCO/SENCOs are still not part of the school's senior management team and have to fit forty-eight hours work into a twenty-four hour day. They are often expected to possess a body of knowledge without the necessary training, and to fulfil their role without adequate resources or facilities.

During 2002 educators, LEA professionals and parents will have to develop an understanding of not only the COP 2002. They will also have to understand the implications of the Special Educational Needs and Disability Act 2001 which will start to bring into force anti-disability discrimination regulations in September 2002. Many professionals will have insufficient training for this task and many will feel threatened by this whole area. People cannot work together when they feel threatened. Adequate training in these areas is essential if we are to solve the problems of our SpLD children.

learning and behavioural difficulties being seen in our student population. (It would also appear that our young children are particularly vulnerable to such exposure.) This is an incredibly contentious issue, for in order for this area to be fully investigated we will have to 'take on' big business – those who make billions of pounds out of providing us with processed food. We may also need to revise our vaccination programme (see Book 5). Over the past ten years there has been a huge rise in Statemented children in the UK accompanied by a rise in both the number of SEN (and behaviourally challenging) students and parents/schools applying for Statements. We will be failing our children (and ourselves) if we do not address these issues. By dealing with the cause we may dramatically reduce the need for provision, with its associated reduction in the financial and emotional costs to society.

All too often professionals are unaware of the plight of (and the trauma being experienced by) parents, adults who have the conditions and their partners. They do not see their tears, they do not see them plucking up their courage in both hands before they approach professionals to ask for help for their child, themselves or their partner.

A rosebud without water or light will fail to thrive. Although full of potential to produce beautiful blossom it will wither and die instead. Human beings also need to thrive – they need to fulfil their potential. Some individuals succeed despite their difficulties, others will fail without support. One cannot support what one does not recognise. Without recognition that a difficulty is present, inappropriate provision may be given or no provision at all.

All people have strengths and weaknesses. Although difficulties exist, they are only part of a person - a part which may have great relevance in certain situations (such as at school and college) but very little in others. Alongside the difficulties, people may have also received 'gifts', which, if enabled to develop, can far exceed the abilities of others. Many have managed to achieve their goals despite their difficulties. Their difficulties may not have disappeared but have been hidden or reduced by their strengths. However, under stress, some, or all, of the difficulties may return. Alternatively, in later life, parents may see similar difficulties affecting their children. So, once again they have to start looking for **solutions** - and so this library was named.

Provision for Specific Learning Difficulties by Jan Poustie   ISBN 1 901544 18 4

APPENDIX 1

Poustie Identification Checklists
PIC 1– 6

These checklists are designed to provide a starting point for those who need to be able to identify the SpLD Profile conditions (e.g. educators, parents and students) so that appropriate provision and referrals for diagnosis to specialist professionals can occur. Principally designed for school age children and adults each checklist explains which items should be used for which students. Primary and secondary children: use all the list. Adults: use items marked # unless told otherwise in the instructions on the checklist. Pre-school (3 - 4 years): use only the shaded items (also see right-hand column below).

Method of use for each of the PIC checklists:

1. Fill in the checklist. Note: each statement has a rating scale (the numbers in the right-hand column) which ranges from 1-5 .
    5= this happens a lot; 1= this happens rarely. Enter the behaviours/ indicators which are present by ticking the appropriate boxes in each checklist. Only tick those behaviours that are present. Circle each of the elements in each question that are present; e.g. in question 1 of PIC 1 (on page 30) if difficulties have been noted in 'organising thoughts' and 'remembering the names of things' then both these phrases should be circled. Parents may now choose to hand in the checklist to the SENCO/AENCO of their child's school.

2. Professionals (and interested parents) should follow the advice at the bottom of the relevant checklists as to which of the book/s in the library should now be read. Thus PIC 1 advises you to read Book 3 of the *Identification Solutions for Specific Learning Difficulties Library*. Each of the books in this library contain additional checklists and a wider range of indicators (including more detailed information of the indicators seen in pre-school children and adults). The books contain instructions for making referrals to the correct medical/educational professionals.

3. Enter the score in the 'results' box. Circle yes or no as appropriate in the 'Results' and 'Is a referral advised' boxes. Always include a copy of the relevant PIC when making a referral.

4. If the student scores positively on the PIC checklist/s and his/her profile matches the information within the relevant books from this library it does not automatically mean that the student has the condition/s. However, there are indications that the condition/s may be present and so a referral for a diagnostic assessment via the student's GP is recommended. If the majority of the statements on a checklist are ticked, then there is a strong possibility that the condition is present. In such cases it is always advised that provision, within an educational and home setting, should be put in to place for the likely condition whilst awaiting for such an assessment to take place. (Note: the individual should be referred to an educational psychologist, the Learning Support Department of the educational establishment or to a SpLD specialist if Dyslexia or Dyscalculia are thought to be present.)

If a behaviour/indicator is not present
Put a long diagonal line through the complete right-hand column; e.g. one line through all the boxes 1 – 5 if the behaviour/indicator is not present.

Assessing 3 - 5 year olds
The reader is advised to refer to *From birth to five years: children's developmental progress* by Mary D Sheridan (ISBN 0415164583, pub. Routledge), along with using the PIC checklists when making an identification of a child aged 3 - 5 years. It is an excellent and easy-to-understand book. It provides information on the developmental stages of children. It covers social behaviour, play, vision, fine movements, hearing, speech, posture and large movements.

© Jan Poustie 2001. *Provision for Specific Learning Difficulties* by Jan Poustie   ISBN 1 901544 18 4

PIC 1: Poustie Identification Checklist for Speech and Language Impairment (3 years to adult)

GENERAL INFORMATION								
Assessor:			Method of Assessment:					
Name of student	Date of Consultation		Student's age		Date of birth			
Results: Number of items scoring between 2 and 6 points = Does the student's profile fit the information in Book 3? Yes/No					Is a referral advised: Yes/No			

Each statement has a rating scale: 5= this happens a lot, 1= this happens rarely. Only tick those behaviours that are present.

	All items may be seen in school age children. Shaded areas = may be seen from 3 years. # = carries on into adulthood.	1	2	3	4	5
A1	Difficulties in expressing what is known and understood (expressive language); e.g. organising one's thoughts, finding the word you want to use from memory, remembering the names of things, starting a conversation and keeping it going. #					
A2	Difficulties in understanding what is heard or read (receptive language); e.g. instructions, understanding the story once you have read/heard it, knowing the meanings of age-appropriate words. #					
A3	Difficulties in paying attention to the sounds in speech; e.g. hearing, attention difficulties; distinguishing or discriminating between speech sounds; hearing the words but having difficulty in understanding: e.g. doing the exact opposite of what s/he was told to do; remembering the sequence of sounds. #					
A4	Slurred speech due to weak or incorrect movements of the speech organs (can be mild to severe). Can affect speech in different ways; e.g. slow and limited in range, fast but cannot be understood. *Many have difficulties in acquiring literacy skills even when early speaking problems have been resolved.* #					
A5	Difficulties in pronouncing some sounds; e.g. 'sh' may be said as 'ch'/'k'					
A6	Speech can be rapid, slow, muddled or slurred. (The listener may not be able to understand it.) #					
A7	Does not have an age appropriate vocabulary and is not understood by everyone s/he speaks to. (By 3 years should have a 200+ word vocabulary and be able to create 4 - 5 word sentences.)					
B1	Difficulties in using grammar correctly; e.g. organising words into the correct sentence order, using verb tenses correctly, learning punctuation. #					
B2	Difficulties in using prepositions (words that tell us the position of a thing in space; e.g. in, on). #					
B3	Difficulties in understanding metaphors and expressions such as 'cut it out' etc. #					
B4	Difficulties in understanding language-based humour (may take offence when people say something as a joke as the student takes the words literally). #					
B5	Difficulties in using higher-level language (e.g. I 'ought to have' mowed the lawn). #					
B6	Difficulties in using language in appropriate settings; e.g. knowing when to use formal language. #					
B7	Difficulties in making sense of language in and out of context. #					
B8	Difficulties in knowing how, and when, to question the information read or listened to. (The person may be unaware that s/he does not understand, so does not ask questions to expand his/her knowledge.) #					
C1	Not paying attention, giving up trying. #					
C2	Misbehaving; e.g. may appear to disobey, may have poor negotiating skills, may argue a lot. #					

Scoring: If the rating is 2-5 for:
▸   two or more of the items in section A (Pre-school students, school age and adult students) or
▸   two or more items in section B (School age and adult students only)
then read Book 3; if the student's profile fits then refer (and complete PIC 6).
A3: if this is present then complete PIC 5 (in this book) and complete PIC 7 which is in Book 3.
C1 - C2: if either of these are ticked then read Book 5.
A1 – A7: If the answer is yes to any of these questions then read Books 3 and 4.

PIC 2: Poustie Identification Checklist for Dyslexia (3 years to adult)

GENERAL INFORMATION			
Assessor:		Method of Assessment:	
Name of student	Date of Consultation	Student's age	Date of birth
Results: Number of items scoring between 2 and 6 points = Does the profile fit the information in Book 4? Yes/No			Is a referral advised: Yes/No

Each statement has a rating scale: 5= this happens a lot, 1= this happens rarely. Only tick those behaviours that are present.

All items may be seen in school age children. Shaded areas = may be seen from 3 years. # = carries on into adulthood.		1	2	3	4	5
A1	A family history of Dyslexia/reading difficulties or other SpLD Profile conditions or the student has coordination difficulties (e.g. Developmental Dyspraxia/DCD) or speech and language difficulties. #					
B1	Confusion in words and actions relating to direction; e.g. knowing which is left/right, up/down. #					
B2	Difficulties in understanding, following or duplicating a sequence; e.g. learning months of the year, learning tables. (In the young child this may be seen as not knowing the name of the next meal; e.g. the child thinks that supper comes after breakfast.) #					
B3	Difficulties in learning nursery rhymes and/or understanding what a rhyme is; e.g. cat, bat, sat. #					
B4	Difficulties in remembering things that s/he has seen (visual) or heard (auditory); e.g. the fine details of the information and the order in which they were presented. (Younger children may have problems with remembering the order of coloured beads on a string, which items are on a tray once they are covered over, the order of sounds in a word.) Some people may have problems in both visual and auditory skills.					
C1	Although the student may like someone reading to him/her, s/he may show little or no interest in reading alone and may dislike/avoid such reading. #					
C2	Repeats phrases/words (or struggles) when reading even when the phrases/words were read correctly the first time. #					
C3	Reads/writes letters/or numerals back to front and upside down this is likely to lead to the child confusing any of the following pairs for each other: 'hy', '69', '25', 'un', 'mw', 'ij' plus all of bdpq can be confused for each other. May also reverse words/letters; e.g. on/no and was/saw. #					
C4	Difficulties in 'proofreading' the student's written work, such that mistakes cannot be seen even when the work is read out to the student. #					
C5	A difference between what the student can say (or knows) about a topic and his/her ability to write or read about it. (Note: that a difference in oral and written/reading ability may not be present if the student has a language impairment.) #					
C6	Works erratically (one minute able to do it and the next unable to do it). #					
C7	Inaccurate reading; e.g. loses place, misses out lines of text/words/phrases, misreads words. #					
C8	Difficulties in learning spellings unless taught using specialist teaching methods; e.g. Fernald method, onset and rime and using the sounds made by the letters/groups of letters to break down/build up words. #					
C9	Problems in understanding what s/he has read. (If this difficulty is present, see Book 3.) #					

Scoring: If the rating is 2-5 for:
▸ two or more of the items in section B (<u>Pre-school, School age and adult students</u>) or
▸ 3 or more items in section C (<u>School age and adult students only</u>)
then read Book 4, if the student's profile fits then refer. A checklist of indicators for adults with Dyslexia can be found on the British Dyslexia Association's infodisk (Section: ato3test).
A1: If this is present, but the student does not meet the criteria for referral, then monitor the student's functioning and progress very carefully plus complete all the checklists in this book.

PIC 3: Poustie Identification Checklist for Dyscalculia (Mathematical Learning Difficulties) 3 yrs-adult

GENERAL INFORMATION			
Assessor:		Method of Assessment:	
Name of student	Date of Consultation	Student's age	Date of birth
Results: Number of items scoring between 2 and 6 points = Does the student's profile fit the information in *Mathematics Solutions: An Introduction to Dyscalculia Part A?* Yes/No			Is a referral advised: Yes/No

Each statement has a rating scale: 5= this happens a lot, 1= this happens rarely. Only tick those behaviours that are present.

All items may be seen in school age children. Shaded areas = may be seen from 3 years. # = carries on into adulthood.		I	2	3	4	5
AI	A family history of Dyslexia/reading difficulties, Dyscalculia/mathematical difficulties or other SpLD Profile conditions or the student has coordination difficulties (e.g. Developmental Dyspraxia/DCD) or speech and language difficulties. #					
A2	Becoming angry/frustrated with any mathematically-based task or game. #					
A3	A dislike of all (or many) leisure games or toys that involve numbers, counting or spatial concepts; e.g. dominoes, snakes and ladders, chess, Connect 4. #					
A4	Combined attention span and information-processing difficulties resulting in slow recall of basic arithmetic facts. May work slowly and erratically. May avoid doing maths and tire easily when attempting mathematical tasks. #					
A5	Failure or difficulties in understanding/using money. May rarely check the change when shopping. #					
A6	Miscounting of objects and/or misreading of text/numerals. #					
A7	Difficulties with understanding and using the language of mathematics. #					
A8	A dislike and/or fear of mathematics or numbers. #					
BI	Difficulties in learning to read the time. #					
B2	Difficulties in fully understanding new concepts unless they are introduced using things that the student can touch and manipulate to work out the answers; e.g. counters, rods). #					
B3	Difficulties in understanding fractions and/or algebra. #					
B4	Difficulties in planning and organising his/her life and his/her environment, and/or a mathematical task. #					
B5	Difficulties in understanding and using statistical information. #					
B6	Frequently pressing the wrong keys on a calculator. #					
B7	Children finding cooking lessons stressful. Adults preferring to cook 'one-pot' meals and meals based on one's own recipes rather than follow recipes in the book. Both groups may have difficulties in modifying the quantities in recipes. #					
CI	Difficulties when travelling; e.g. going to the wrong platform, finding it difficult to read a map, forgetting road numbers etc. #					
C2	Difficulties with working out how much wallpaper/paint etc. is needed for a DIY task. #					
C3	Frequently missing appointments due to writing details down incorrectly and/or a poor sense of time. #					

Scoring: If the rating is 2 –5 for:
➡ three or more items in section A and two or more items in section B (<u>School age to adult students</u>)
➡ 2 or more of the shaded items <u>Pre-school children</u>)
then read *Mathematics Solutions: An Introduction to Dyscalculia: Part A* by Jan Poustie, published by Next Generation, ISBN 1901544 451. If the profile fits then refer. (Note: section C applies to older students and adults only.)

PIC 4: Poustie Identification Checklist for
Developmental Dyspraxia/DCD/Motor Coordination Difficulties (3 years to adult)

GENERAL INFORMATION			
Assessor:		Method of Assessment:	
Name of student	Date of Consultation	Student's age	Date of birth
Results: Number of items scoring between 2 and 6 points = Does the student's profile fit the information in Book 6? Yes/No			Is a referral advised: Yes/No

Each statement has a rating scale: 5= this happens a lot, 1= this happens rarely. Only tick those behaviours that are present.

	All items may be seen in school age children. Shaded areas = may be seen from 3 years, # = carries on into adulthood.	1	2	3	4	5
A1	Poor balancing skills; e.g. may have difficulties in learning to roller blade, to ride a tricycle/bike. #					
A2	Difficulties in remembering and carrying out motor-based tasks. #					
A3	Difficulties relating to spatial awareness and judging distances; e.g. may have problems with catching a ball, may put mugs too close to the edge of a table, may knock into things. #					
A4	Lack of coordination between the two sides of the body; e.g. may find it difficult to learn to play musical instruments and to swim. #					
A5	Poor planning and organisational skills or emotional immaturity as compared with peer group. May become easily distressed. #					
A6	Clumsiness; e.g. may press too hard and break things, knock into people and objects. #					
A7	Poor presentation of work/self. May look untidy and work may be untidy. #					
A8	Sensory hypo/hypersensitivity. Any of the following may be present: may actively dislike certain noises, textures of cloth, textures in the mouth, sensations (e.g. dislike of having hair cut, teeth cleaned), people being too close to them (including a dislike of crowds) or tight clothes. #					
A9	Fidgeting, restlessness. (May prefer to lie down rather than sit when doing homework.) #					
B1	Difficulties in finding things against a busy background; e.g. difficulties in finding an item on a notice board or in a drawer with any ease. #					
B2	Poor and/or slow handwriting. #					
B3	Difficulties in doing tasks which need good control over fingers (fine motor control) or spatial skills; e.g. dressing, tying shoelaces, writing, drawing, using cutlery. #					
B4	Difficulties in reading, writing or spelling. #					
B5	Sucking, swallowing, and chewing difficulties; difficulties in learning to blow his/her nose; speech and/or language difficulties. #					
B6	Difficulties in mathematics, dislike playing games that use numbers or spatial skills. #					
B7	Difficulties in carrying out a sequence of actions; e.g. the correct sequence for threading a sewing machine, doing up buttons, putting on a coat. #					

Scoring: If the rating is 2-5 for two or more of the items in section A or B (Pre-school, School age and adult students) read Book 6, if the student's profile fits then refer (also read Book 1).
If the rating is 2-5 for: ,
▷▷ **A9:** read Books 1, 5 and 6,

▷▷ **B2 or B3:** read Books 4 and 6,
▷▷ **B4:** read Books 1, 3 and 4,
▷▷ **B5:** read Books 3 and 6,
▷▷ **B6:** read *Mathematics Solutions Part A by Jan Poustie et al* ISBN 1 901544 45 1.

PIC 5: Poustie Identification Checklist for Attention Deficits Hyperactivity Disorder (3 years to adult)
(Including the criteria used by the AD/HD Family Support Group UK)

GENERAL INFORMATION				
Assessor:		Method of Assessment:		
Name of student	Date of Consultation	Student's age		Date of birth
Results: Number of items scoring between 2 and 6 points = Does s/he meet the method 2 criteria (page 35) or does his/her profile fit the information in Book 5? Yes/No				Is a referral advised: Yes/No

Each statement has a rating scale: 5= this happens a lot, 1= this happens rarely. Only tick those behaviours that are present.

All items apply to school age children. B4 may not apply to all adults. Shaded areas = may be seen from 3 years.		1	2	3	4	5
Section A. ATTENTION DIFFICULTIES						
A1	Makes careless mistakes/does not give close attention to details. (May miss out numbers in sums, miss out letters in words, misread symbols etc.) #					
A2	Has difficulty concentrating on tasks or play activities (though if interested in the task s/he may be able to concentrate for a long time and is likely to resent having to leave the task). #					
A2	Does not seem to listen to what is being said to him or her. #					
A3	Is easily distracted by extraneous stimuli; (e.g. distracted by noises and movements within a classroom/nursery, the pictures on the wall, or even his/her own thoughts; sensory integration difficulties may also be present, see Book 6.) #					
A4	Understands instructions but has difficulty in carrying them out. #					
A5	Avoids/dislikes/or is reluctant to do tasks, especially those that s/he finds boring, or tasks that require sustained mental effort. (If the task involves mental effort s/he is likely to work better in a quiet environment. A child may leave homework until the last minute and may need a parent to keep him/her company. The child may need one-to-one attention in a classroom in order to start and finish tasks.) #					
A6	Has difficulties in organising tasks and activities. (Will be present in the pre-school child but tends to be more easily spotted in the school child and adults.) #					
A7	Often loses things necessary for tasks or activities at school/home/work; (e.g. toys, pencils, books, mobile phones). #					
A8	Engages in physically dangerous activities without considering possible consequences. (This is not done to gain thrills but s/he appears to be unaware of the consequences of his/her actions; e.g. runs into the street without looking. Adults may be aware of risks but ignore them.) #					
A9	Forgets things when doing daily activities; (e.g. may forget to turn up for a lesson or a meeting). #					
A10	May have great difficulty in starting tasks. (This can occur even though s/he knows, and accepts, that the task has to be done.) #					
A11	Daydreams when s/he should be doing another task. #					
A12	Fails to finish tasks. (May move from one uncompleted task to another. May be very keen to learn a skill; e.g. play a musical instrument but easily loses motivation to learn it unless the skill comes very easily to him/her.) #					
A13	Exhibits anxiety. (e.g. may be worried about not getting tasks done but still fails to do them. The child may be worried about getting told off in playgroup or in school; (e.g., told off about getting his/her work completed to the teacher's satisfaction.) The child's behaviour is his/her way of demonstrating the anxiety.) #					

Each statement has a rating scale: 5= this happens a lot, 1= this happens rarely. Only tick those behaviours that are present.						
All items may be seen in school age children and adults. Shaded areas = may be seen from 3 years.		1	2	3	4	5
Section B. HYPERACTIVITY and IMPULSIVITY						
HYPERACTIVITY						
B1	Fidgets with hands or feet and/or may squirm in seat. *(In adolescence and adulthood the student may feel restless instead.)* #					
B2	Has difficulty remaining seated when required to do so; *(e.g. in the classroom, at the dinner table; in adulthood this may show as feelings of restlessness).* #					
B3	Runs and/or climbs in situations where it is inappropriate to do so. *(Any of the following can be seen; inappropriate behaviours in school; e.g. may climb up the ropes in the gym whilst waiting for P.E. lesson to start . Toddlers may learn to climb before they can walk. Young children may run without thought of danger or of the fact that their parents are now out of sight.)*					
B4	Has difficulty playing (or taking part in a leisure activity) quietly. *(Parents, teachers and partners may find the student unrelaxing and noisy to be with, though in periods of great concentration these students may be very quiet..)*					
B5	Has unusually high levels of activity *(e.g. like a clock-work toy with no off switch!).* #					
B6	Talks too much. *(This may be the student's way of expressing his/her thoughts as there can be an immaturity in the student's ability to internalise thoughts so they 'talk it through'.)* #					
IMPULSIVITY						
B7	Blurts out the answers before questions have been completed. #					
B8	Has difficulty waiting for his/her turn, in games or other group situations. *(May push other children out of the way to get to a toy, may not see the need to queue, adults may hate queuing. May become very frustrated if s/he cannot say what s/he wants to say now. May become distressed/angry if you postpone tasks and activities.. May ignore/be unaware of the needs of others.)* #					
B9	Interrupts conversations and other people's activities. *(So, may barge his/her way across a board game that other children are playing. Both adults and children may interrupt conversations. Adults may interrupt a colleague in the middle of an explanation or the speaker at a lecture..)* #					

Scoring (for students of all ages):
Method 1: If two or more elements from sections B or C (or three or more elements from section A) are present, then read Book 5, if the student's profile fits then refer the student for assessment (also read Books 1 and 6).

Method 2: If the following statements are true then you can refer without reading Book 5 (although it is strongly recommended that you also read Book 5 as well):
▸▸   6 or more indicators in section A are ticked.
▸▸   5 or more indicators in section B are ticked.
▸▸   Some or all of these indicators have been present before the age of seven years.
▸▸   The behaviours are seen in more than one setting (e.g. at school, at home, with the grandparents, with friends, at work, when involved in leisure activities outside of the home etc.)
▸▸   The student's behaviours are affecting his/her social, academic functioning or his/her functioning at work (e.g. socially the student may have few friends/be known by all but not a popular member of the class.)

Referral: This is usually made via the student's GP to the NHS professional in your area who specialises in ADHD.
If either A3 or A4 is present then read Book 3 and complete the Auditory Processing Disorder checklist at the back of it.

PIC 6: Poustie Identification Checklist for Autistic Spectrum Disorder (3 years to adult)

GENERAL INFORMATION				
Assessor:			Method of Assessment:	
Name of student	Date of Consultation		Student's age	Date of birth
Results: Number of items scoring between 2 and 6 points = Does the student's profile fit the information in Book 5? Yes/No			Is a referral advised: Yes/No	

Each statement has a rating scale: 5= this happens a lot, 1= this happens rarely. Only tick those behaviours that are present.

	ASD indicators change over time and may be less obvious in very structured settings and in adults/higher functioning students. Item B1 will always apply. Items B6 and C4 may apply to some pre-school students.	1	2	3	4	5
1	Repetitive behaviours/movements (e.g. spinning) may self-harm (e.g. head banging) rigid in activities (e.g. no changes can be made), obsessional interest in one topic or aspect of the topic. #					
A. Difficulties with social interaction						
A1	Often appears aloof and indifferent to other people. (Note: attachment may be shown to parents/carers, may enjoy certain forms of active physical contact). #					
A2	Accepts social contact but does so in a passive way. (May even show some signs of pleasure in this but does not makes spontaneous approaches.) #					
A2	Approaches other people in an odd, inappropriate, repetitive way. (Pays little/no attention to the responses of those s/he approaches.) Interactions may be inappropriately stilted and over formal.#					
A3	Interactions may be inappropriately stilted and over formal with family/friends/strangers.#					
B. Difficulties with social communication (verbal and non-verbal)						
B1	Does not understand the social uses of (or find pleasure in) communication. (Some may have lots to say but they talk 'at' others and not 'with' them.) #					
B2	Does not understand that language is a tool for conveying information to others. (The person may be able to ask for his/her own needs but finds it hard to talk about feelings or thoughts.) #					
B3	Does not understand the emotions, ideas and beliefs of other people. (Is not able to see something from another person's point of view.) #					
B4	Difficulties in understanding (or giving) information via gestures, facial expressions or tone of voice. (May use gestures but these tend to be odd and inappropriate.)#					
B5	Literal use/understanding of language; (if you say 'its raining cats and dogs' will look for the animals!).#					
B6	Uses an idiosyncratic, pompous, choice of words and phrases. Content of speech will be limited. (May be fascinated with words but does not use his/her vocabulary when interacting socially.) #					
C. Difficulties with imagination (affects play, written work etc.)						
C1	Does not play imaginatively with objects or toys, or with other children or adults. (A child may appear to be playing imaginatively by copying story lines from favourite stories etc. Will not be able to pretend; e.g. cannot pretend that a paintbrush is a car and move it round a track.)					
C2	Tendency to focus on minor/trivial things around him/her or an element of a thing rather than the whole thing. (So, the younger student may focus on a ring rather than the person wearing it.) #					
C4	Misses the point of activities that involve words; e.g. social conversation, literature (especially fiction) and subtle verbal humour. #					
C5	Cannot use past and present events to predict consequences or as a basis for planning the future. #					

Scoring (for students of all ages): If the rating is 2-5 for one or more items in each of sections A, B and C then read
- Book 5, if the student's profile fits then refer (also read Book 1).
- Read Books 3 and 5 if two or more elements of section B are ticked.
- Read Book 3 if C4 is ticked.
- If B3 or B4 is present, then read Book 5.

APPENDIX 2: Help and Support

(Each book of the library also contains Help and Support sections.)

SpLD SUPPORT

Each of these national bodies will be able to tell you the contact details of your local group. If you live outside of the UK then contact the relevant UK agency and ask for the details of your country's organisation.

The ADHD Family Support Group UK
c/o Mrs G Mead, 1A High St, Dilton Marsh, Westbury, Wiltshire BA13 4DL. Tel: 01373 826 045.

The Hyperactive Children's Support Group
71 Whyke Lane, Chichester, West Sussex PO19 2LD. Tel/Fax: 01903 725182.

ADDISS
PO Box 340, Middlesex, HA8 9HL Tel: 0208 905 2013; Fax: 0208 386 6466. Stocks ADD/ADHD books.

The British Dyslexia Association
98 London Road, Reading, RG1 5AU. Helpline: 0118 966 8271; Website: http://www.bda-dyslexia.org.uk./

Dyspraxia Foundation
8 West Alley, Hitchin, Herts United Kingdom SG5 1EG. Tel: 01462 454 986; Fax: 01462 455 052.

AFASIC – Association For All Speech Impaired Children
69–85 Old Street, London EC1V 9HX. Tel: 020 7841 8900.

The National Autistic Society
393 City Road, London EC1V 1NE. Tel: 020 7833 2299, Fax: 0171 833 9666.

TEACHING ORGANISATIONS

PATOSS (Professional Association of Teachers of Students with SpLD)
PO Box 66, Cheltenham, Gloucestershire, GL53 9YF.

NASEN (National Association for Special Educational Needs)
NASEN House, 4/5 Amber Business Village, Amber Close, Amington, Tamworth, Staffs, B77 4RP, Tel: 01827 311500. Produces a wide range of useful books and holds conferences. They publish three journals *British Journal of Special Education, Support for Learning* and *Special*. Membership is open to professionals, parents etc.

OTHER ORGANISATIONS

National Association for Gifted Children
Suite 14, Challenge House, Sherwood Drive, Bletchley, Milton Keynes. Tel: 08707703217. Website: www.nagcbritain.org.uk
E-mail: amazingchildren@nagcbritain.org.uk

Institute of Neuro-physiological Psychology
Warwick House, 4 Stanley Place, Chester
Tel: 01244 311414
Provides training for Neuro-developmental Delay.

The Society of Homeopaths
4A Artizan Road, Northampton, NN1 4HU.
Tel. 01604 621400, Fax: 01604 622622.
Website: www.homepathy-soh.org
Provide information leaflets and a list of qualified professional homeopaths if you send an SAE. Some practices now run paediatric clinics. Homeopathic treatments can be of great benefit to individuals whose SpLD causes them severe stress and anxiety/poor sleep.

British Acupuncture Council
63 Jeddo Road, W12 9HQ, Tel: 0208 7350400. ·
Fax: 020 87350404, Website: www.acupuncture.org.uk

Register of Chinese Herbal Medicine
Office 5, Ferndale Business Centre, 1 Exeter Street, Norwich, NR2 FQB. Tel: 01603 6239944, Fax: 01603 667557

Institute of Complementary Medicine
PO Box 194, London, SE16 1QZ,
Tel: 0207 2375165, Website: www.icmedicine.co.uk

British School of Reflexology
92 Sheering Road, Old Harlow, Essex, CM17 0JW.
Tel: 01279 429060, Fax: 01279 445234
Website: www.footreflexology.com

Shiatsu Society
Eastlands Court, St Peters Road, Rugby, CV21 3QP.
Tel: 01788 555051, Fax: 01788 555052 Website: www.shiatsu.org

Transcendental Meditation
Freepost, London, SW1P 4YY. Tel: 0800 269303.

Migraine Action Association
178a High Road, Byfleet, West Byfleet, Surrey, KT14 7ED, Tel: 01932 352468
Offers useful advice. Signs of a migraine are a headache with some or all of the following: a deep throbbing in the head; a pain on the side of the head; feeling sick or vomiting; being unable to continue with normal activities; seeing flashes, zigzags or objects as being dark, which may be patterned or strange; seeing only part of your environment (as though your eyes have a shutter across part of them); a desire to avoid light and noise; changes in sense of smell; feeling unwell after movement, a dislike of being touched; a desire to be alone; the need to go to bed.

GENERAL SUPPORT
It would be ideal if the details of the organisations in this section were displayed by all of us working in this field. Many of our SpLD students (and possibly their parents/spouses) may not be able to access information via the normal routes; e.g. leaflets. The impact of undiagnosed or unprovided for SpLD can be great. There have been tragic cases of children committing suicide because of their SpLD (parents too may reach breaking point).

Samaritans
General office: 10 The Grove, Slough, Berks, SL1 1QP.
Tel: 01753 532713, Helpline: 08457 909090.
Offers support to those in distress who feel suicidal or despairing, and who need to talk with someone.

Childline
Royal Mail Building, Studd Street, London, N1 0QW.
Tel: 0207 239 1000, Fax: 0207 239 1001
Free helpline for children in trouble or in danger.

Community Drug Project
9a Brockley Cross, Brockley, London, SE4 2AB.
Tel: 0208 692 4975, Fax: 0208 692 996. Provides support within Lewisham area and referral elsewhere.

Depression Alliance
38 Westminster Bridge Road, London, SE1 7JB.
Tel: 0207 633 0557, Fax: 0207 633 0559.
Publish booklets including *Depression in Children and Young People*, *Self Help* and *Student Survival*.

MIND
15–19 Broadway, London, E15 4BQ. Tel: 0208 519 2122.
Produces useful booklets that deal with stress and depression including *Understanding Childhood Stress* and *How to Recognise the Early Signs of Mental Distress*.

Anti-Bullying Campaign
185 Tower Bridge Road, London SE1 2UF.
Tel/Fax: 0207 378 1446. This organisation provides advice, information, understanding and support to parents of bullied children and to children themselves.

BATIAS Advocacy Service
Tel: 01375 392253.

Disability Advocacy Service
Contact: Shirley Gray or Rachel Griffiths
Tel: 01273 720972.

David Shepherd Associates
Carsington, Derbyshire. Tel: 01629 540815.
Specialists in Mental Health Law and Practice.

IPSEA (Independent Panel For Special Education Advice)
6 Carlow Mews, Woodbridge, Suffolk
IP12 1EA. Tel/Fax: 01394 380518, www.ipsea.org.uk
Guides parents through the assessment and tribunal procedures. It can represent parents at SEN tribunals.

Contact a family
170 Tottenham Court Road, London, W1P 0HA
Tel: 0207 383 3555, Fax. 0207 383 0259.
Provides support for families who care for children with disabilities and special needs. Publications include *Siblings and Special Needs* and *A Parent's Guide to Statements of Special Educational Needs in England and Wales*.

SKILL
(The National Bureau for Students with Disabilities.)
This has helpful general information especially about allowances for disabled students. Tel: 0800 328 5050 (1.30–4.30 pm weekdays). Fax: 020 7450 0650, Website: www.skill.org.uk

RELATIONSHIPS
British Association of Psychotherapists
37 Mapesbury Road, London, NW2 4HJ.
Tel: 0208 4529823, Fax: 0208 4525182.
Website: www.bap-psychotherapy.org

British Association for Counselling and Psychotherapy
1 Regent Place, Rugby, CV21 2PJ. Tel.: 0870 4435252.
Fax: 0870 4435160, Website: www.bacp.co.uk

Relate
Herbert Gray College, Little Church Street, Rugby, CV21 3AP, Tel: 01788 573241.
Fax: 01788 535007, Website: www.relate.org.uk

Association of Clinical Hypnotherapists
15 Connaught Square, Marble Arch, London, W2 2HG, Tel: 0207 4029037, Fax: 0207 2621237.

The Education Law Association
37D Grimston Avenue, Folkstone CT20 2QD
Tel/Fax: 01303 211570 E-mail: elassec@btinternet.com
Provides contact details of legal/educational and support and training/networking in education and law.

Appendix 3: Supplementary information
including the Code of Practice 2002 (COP 2002)

All COP 2002 quotes in this appendix are from the Special Educational Needs Code of Practice ISBN 1841855294, published by The Department for Education and Skills (DfES) www.dfes.gov.uk COP 2002 was published in November 2001 but came into force on 1st January 2002 when it replaced the Code of Practice on the Identification and Assessment of Special Educational Needs (referred to in this book as COP 1994). This long document includes information for both parents and professionals, for a free copy ring: 0845 6022260. Additional guidance to the COP 2002 is provided in the form of the SEN Toolkit, ISBN 1841855316 (pub. DfES). Wales: The National Assembly of Wales have published their own version in Welsh and in English with the main content being the same as the COP 2002. This document was published in the Spring of 2002 (See www.wales.gov.uk or Tel: 0292082 5111 for information on this). Scotland: Scottish schools are expected to be aware of the COP 2002.

The COP 2002

The new Code incorporates the effects of the SEN sections of the Special Educational Needs and Disability Act 2001. (A new Disability Rights Code of Practice for Schools will be published, and will co-exist with the COP 2002.) There is a strong emphasis on inclusion in the COP 2002 and a greater emphasis (than in COP 1994) on the importance of parents and the importance of working with them in a full and genuine partnership. Enabling the child to participate from a very early age in the education process (and be consulted whenever possible throughout all SEN processes and procedures including reviews) is a essential part of the COP 2002's guidance. There is also a greater emphasis that ALL teachers are teachers of SEN pupils not just those who work in the Learning Support Department .

Identification, assessment and provision are looked at with relation to the three educational settings (Early Education, Primary Phase and Secondary Sector) with each having their own chapter in the Code. There is a focus in these sections on teaching, learning and achievement. Chapters seven and eight are devoted to Statutory Assessment and the awarding of a Statement of Special Educational Needs. These two chapters state the deadlines which the LEA have to obey for each aspect of the process. Chapter 9 of the Code now includes the role of the Connexions Service (the renamed Careers Service) when the student is making the transition from school to further education.

References from page vi

1. "The key test of the need for action is evidence that current rates of progress are inadequate." (COP 2002, para. 5:41). "To help identify pupils who may have special educational needs, schools can measure children's progress by referring to:
- evidence from teacher observation and assessment
- their performance against the level descriptions within the National Curriculum at the end of a key stage
- their progress against the objectives specified in the

National Literacy and Numeracy Strategy Frameworks
- standardised screening or assessment tools. (COP 2002, para. 6:12.)
2. COP 2002, para. 7:65.
3. COP 2002, para. 7:66.
4. COP 2002, para. 8:36.
5. COP 2002, para. 8:37.
6. COP 2002, para. 8:38.

References from Chapter 1: Provision

1. The aim of the Disagreement Resolution Service is "to prevent the development of long-term problems thus reducing, in time, the number of appeals going to the SEN Tribunal." (COP 2002, para. 2:26). These services should: "demonstrate independence and credibility in working towards early and informal resolution of disagreements."
(COP 2002, para. 2:24)
2. "Meeting the needs of children and young people with SEN successfully requires partnership between all those involved" [including the parents] and that this "depends on clarity of information, good communication and transparent policies." (COP 2002, para: 1:7).
3. The government says that it does not expect "that the various parties would require legal representation at this stage; that would be contrary to the spirit of informal disagreement resolution." (COP 2002, para. 2:27).

Chapter 2: Gaining Provision

Glossary of terms
SENCO/AENCO
The school's SENCO (Special Educational Needs Coordinator) was appointed as a result of the 1994 Code of Practice (COP 1994). Sometimes this professional is called an AENCO (Additional Educational Needs Coordinator). The AENCO role is seen by some as being wider than that of the SENCO role but in some schools both roles will include areas that some people do not always associate with Special Educational Needs;

e.g. English as a Second Language students and gifted students.

<u>EPs/SENST</u>
All Local Educational Authorities (LEAs) employ a group of Educational Psychologists (EPs) and a Special Educational Needs Support Team (SENST/SENS), each of which is allocated a number of LEA schools with which to liaise and assess the school's students as necessary. It should be noted that schools usually only have a budget for a limited number of EP assessments per term.

<u>Very severe SpLD</u>
Usually this includes those whose functioning is within the second percentile (centile). If a student is at the second percentile for reading there will only be two children out of hundred (of his age) who are worse than him at reading.

Implementation of the COP 2002

All schools, early education settings, LEAs and those who help them (e.g. social and health services) must have regard to the COP 2002. However, they only have a legal duty to obey the parts which are placed in the boxes throughout the text. (The foreword of the COP 2002 explains which sections of various UK Acts and Regulations these boxes refer to.) The rest of the COP 2002 is just guidance for good practice with much of it stating what (rather than how) actions should be taken. The inclusion of words/phrases such as 'appropriate', 'progress', 'significant difficulties' and 'graduated response' are very open to different interpretation and so may result in conflict between the various parties involved with the student.

As this book goes to print implementation of the COP 2002 is still in its infancy. Although all SENCOs/AENCOs will have had training in the use of the COP 1994, few will have had much training in the COP 2002 when it comes into force. Some may well feel that the training they have received is inadequate and that they still do not understand it well enough. (They may therefore feel insecure about using it.) Its complexity may make the teacher want to completely bypass its guidance sections. The parental demands for recognition and provision for the child and/or parental knowledge of the COP 2002 may only inflame the situation and increase that insecurity. Note: *The SEN Toolkit* (ISBN 1841855316) which accompanies the COP 2002 and the *Access to education for children and young people with medical needs (ISBN 1 841856223)* provide examples of good practice.

Sometimes LEAs ignore their legal duties; e.g. regarding time limits during the multidisciplinary assessment process. The SEN Tribunal does not concern itself with

this issue but the Local Government Ombudsman does (see bottom of this page).

Making a complaint

Parents can feel very vulnerable when they make a complaint. Complaining is a bit of a 'catch 22' situation. Many find themselves in the position that if they do not complain then they will not get the provision but complaining can result in professionals feeling that they are being backed into a corner and the situation can then become even more difficult. It is a bit like being the victim of a bully, one fears that if one complains then the bullying may worsen. However, no-one can do anything about the bullying until they have been alerted to it. Options 3 and 5 below may result in you having more publicity than you want (and may backfire on you) but in some cases this may be the only way to actually get anything done. There are several other methods (besides those mentioned on pages 15-17) that parents can use to complain about their child's provision.

1. Appeal to the Department of Education and Skills for help (Tel: 0870 0002288). Ask to speak to the Manager of their Special Needs Department, explain the problem. Ask her to become involved in your case. If she shares your concerns then she will refer you to one of her staff who will contact the LEA.
2. Complain (in writing) to the school's governors.
3. Get your local MP involved with the case.
4. Write to the Head of your LEA's Education Department
5. Write to the Chair of the Education Committee. (Ring up your LEA and ask to speak to a person in the department that deals with councillors.) You have to complain to a councillor before you can complain to the Local Government Ombudsman.
6. Complain to the Local Government Ombudsman.
7. Apply for resolution of your problem to the LEAs Disagreement Resolution Service (see COP 2002 2:22 to 2:30 and Section 3 of the SEN Toolkit).

Complaining to the Local Government Ombudsman

Parents who feel that the LEA have acted illegally; e.g. that they have exceeded the time limits for the different stages of the assessment/Statementing process can make a complaint to the Local Government Ombudsman (LGO). First of all they have to take the case as far as they can; e.g. there is an expectation by the LGO that they will take the case to the SEN Tribunal first; e.g. to appeal against the LEA's decision not to assess or

Statement. The LGO cannot challenge the decision of the SEN tribunal but they can look into the way that the LEA handled any of the issues. In order to see whether it is a complaint that the LGO can investigate they would need to have the complaint put into writing. This can be either via a letter or an e-mail to the Local Government Ombudsman, 21 Queen Anne's Gate, London SW1H 9BU. To e-mail them go to their website (www.lgo.org.uk) where there is link to their e-mail facility so you can e-mail your complaint. Note: you have to use their complaint form to make your complaint. (This short form is on their internet site.)

The LGO will then decide whether the complaint is within their jurisdiction and if so they would begin the investigation. The LGO can recommend what the LEA should do to remedy the situation but they cannot force the LEA to comply with their recommendations. If the LEA refuses to comply then the LGO will 'name and shame' them in the hope that they will comply. First they will produce a report (usually accompanied by a press release) which then becomes a public document and is made available to the press, parents etc. If the LEA still refuse to comply then the LEA have to fund the LGO to publish the reasons why the LEA were at fault in the LEA's local press. The LGO find that it is becoming more common for LEAs to comply with their recommendations. However, it is appalling that the LGO service has been set up as 'a paper tiger' in that the LEA can actually get away with acting illegally without having to make reddress to the parents/student.

OFSTED
Alexandra House, 29-33 Kingsway, London WC2B 6SE, Tel: 0207 4216800, Fax: 0207 4216707, Helpline: 0207 4216673.

All parents should be given a summary version of the school's OFSTED report and they (and every person who works at the school) should receive a full copy of the School's Action Plan that follows it. They are also entitled to see the full copy of the report, which is held at the school. The Code recommends that the Action Plan is reported on every year at the Annual Parent's Meeting. A full copy of the OFSTED report and the School's Action Plan are kept in the local public library or can be seen on the Ofsted website: www.ofsted.gov.uk/inspect/index.htm

References from Chapter 2
1. COP 2002, para. 1:14.
2. COP 2002, para. 4:27.
3. COP 2002, para. 2:24 "demonstrate independence

and credibility in working towards early and informal resolution of disagreements."
4. COP 2002, "All children should be involved in making decisions where possible right from the start of their education." (para. 3:6) "They should feel confident that they will be listened to and that their views are valued." (para. 3:2) "Their perceptions and experiences can be invaluable to professionals in reaching decisions." (para. 3:3).
5. COP 2002, paras. 3:6 - 3:10.
6. "LEAs, schools and settings should show sensitivity, honesty and mutual respect in encouraging pupils to share concerns, discuss strategies and see themselves as equal partners with the school." (COP 2002, para. 3:5)
7. "Children, who are capable of forming views, have a right to receive and make known information, to express an opinion, and to have that opinion taken into account in any matters affecting them. The views of the child should be given due weight according to the age, maturity and capability of the child. See Articles 12 and 13, The United Nations Convention on the Rights of the Child." (Key statutory duties box at the head of Section 3 COP 2002.)
8. COP 2002, para. 7:85.
9. "a significantly greater difficulty in learning than the majority of children of the same age." (COP 2002, key statutory duties box bottom of page 6, referring to Section 312, Education Act 1996.)
10. "The Code sets out guidance on policies and procedures aimed at enabling pupils with special educational needs (SEN) to reach their full potential, to be included fully in their school communities and make a successful transition to adulthood." (COP 2002, para. 1:2)
11. COP 2002, para. 2:6 "Positive attitudes to parents, user-friendly information and procedures and awareness of support needs are important. There should be no presumption about what parents can or cannot do to support their children's learning. Stereotypic views of parents are unhelpful and should be challenged. All staff should bear in mind the pressures a parent may be under because of the child's needs."
12. COP 2002, para. 7:24
13. COP 2002, para. 7:25.
14. COP 2002, para. 7:4.
15. COP 2002, para. 7:23.
16. "must have regard to it. They must not ignore it." (COP 2002, Foreword para. 5, page iii)
17. COP 2002, para. 1:6 states as two of the factors

critical for success that:
"special education professionals and parents work in partnership, special education professionals take into account the views of individual parents in respect of their child's particular needs."

18. COP 2002, para. 2:7 states that:
"To make communications effective professionals should: acknowledge and draw on parental knowledge and expertise in relation to their child."

19. "Head teachers should also ensure where possible that the SENCO is able to communicate with other SENCOs through, for example, the SENCO Forum coordinated by the British Educational and Technology Communications Agency (BECTa). (COP 2002, para. 5:36.)

20. COP 2002, para. 2:21 includes as one of the minimum standards to be provided by Parent Partnership Services "that training on good communication and relationships with parents is made available to teachers, governors and staff in SEN sections of the LEA."

21. Of equal importance is the training of school and LEA staff on "consulting children and young people with communication difficulties" (COP 2002, para. 3:22). Also see para. 2:7 (6th bullet point) reference dealing with parents who have similar difficulties.

Word from the author

SEN/SpLD provision throughout the whole school: In some schools the staff of the Learning Support Department (LSD) may be excellent. However, the school's special needs provision may virtually not exist outside of the LSD. This is more likely to occur once the student has left primary school as all too often secondary school subject teachers view SEN as a matter for others and not themselves. Subject teachers need to be aware that the COP 2002 (paras. 5:2 and 6:2) states that 'all teachers are teachers of pupils with special educational needs.' Innovative ways of encouraging a change of attitude need to be explored by head teachers. The author was once in the splendid situation where, as Head of a secondary school LSD, she was given extra budget. All departments could apply for some of the budget as long as they liaised with her to ensure that it was spent on SEN within their subject.

The importance of diet: In Book 1 of the library dietary issues such as essential fatty acids deficiency (which are usually removed from processed foods), high sugar, high saturated fat, mineral impoverished diets, caffeine loaded diets and their effect upon mental functioning and behaviour was raised. (This is further explored in

Appendix 3 and also in Book 5 of this library.) Caffeine is likely to become a big issue in our schools, The author is already aware of students who deliberately change their diet so that they go on 'caffeine highs'. (They do not eat before school and then buy the right items from their school snack dispensing machines. As a result they become unteachable for the rest of the day.) It is not always easy to recognise caffeine in a list of ingredients for the herb guarana (which the author has noted being added to some soft drinks) also contains caffeine.

Advice from external specialists: The COP 2002 (in para 7:35 which relates to the evidence for deciding whether to make a statutory assessment) specifically mentions that 'LEAs should pay particular attention to ... evidence provided by ... the parents and other professionals where they have been involved with the child.' If the COP 2002 regards such evidence as acceptable during this part of a legal process then it must be acceptable throughout the child's educational career. LEA staff and schools need up-to-date guidelines advising them of which qualifications are acceptable from outside professionals. Educators who do not know what a qualification means have no idea as to whether the report in their hand should be acted upon.

Offending and learning difficulties: In a report on HM Prison Wayland in 1999 Sir David Ramsbotham (Her Majesty's ex-Chief Inspector of Prisons) stated that 'all the evidence points to the connection between education and recidivism' [reoffending]. There is some evidence that the proportion of prisoners with literacy difficulties reflects the social class composition of the prison population. (See A *Survey of reading ability in prisons* produced by the Institute of Criminology, www.yearofreading.org.uk/Database/prisonsurvey.html) However, this proportion of prisoners may actually be a reflection of the fact that there is a genetic/inheritance factor in the SpLD Profile conditions (e.g. Dyslexia is known to be eighty per cent inherited). It is very difficult for individuals to improve their circumstances (e.g. move to a higher social class) via improved skills/qualifications, leading to better employment, unless they can read. Thus in each generation we are likely to see children (especially from the poorer sections of our society) having the same struggle to gain qualifications as their parents. It is therefore only too easy to see the poverty (or social welfare) as being the cause of the difficulties rather than seeing that the cause is the SpLD Profile conditions themselves. The net result is that our SpLD Profile children may not receive the provision needed until the family has managed to improve its social position - and then we can see the middle-class anxious parent feared/disliked by so many teachers who makes provision happen!

APPENDIX 4: Intervention from the child's point of view

The following information is derived from the statistics found in Fact File 2000 (ISBN 1 872365 56 6) which is updated on a yearly basis. It is published by Carel Press, 4 Hewson St., Carlisle CA2 5AU, Tel: 01228 538928   Fax: 01228 591816 Carel_Press@compuserve.com

There is a tendency for some to think of intervention in terms of a worksheet or another resource that we would use with the student including using the checklist sheets (appropriate to the condition) found in this book. However, that form of intervention is starting from the condition and the problems it presents rather than starting from the student. It is perhaps easier for an adult to tell us what s/he needs in the way of general needs than it is for a child.

The COP 2002 (section 3, and the SEN Toolkit, section 4) provides detailed information on the need to involve the student when deciding SEN provision. The following information found in the section *What children say about school 1 and 2* (on pages 62/63 of the above mentioned book) provides us with an insight into the mind of the child. Five hundred questionnaires were sent out to primary and secondary schools in one education authority in the North West of England at the end of June 1998. By the end of July 1998 two thousand, five hundred and twenty-seven returns had been received from children ranging from those in reception class to those in the final year at secondary school. The answers were derived from the children's responses to questions about school.

(The source of the information was the Bolton Data for Inclusions, Bolton Institute 1998.)

The main factors relating to whether a child was happy or unhappy at school are shown below.

What makes a good teacher?
53.9% Happy, kind and understanding
27.2% Respectful and fair
9.2% Creative
9.1 % Doesn't shout

What makes a bad teacher?
44.2% Shouts, bad tempered
26.8% Too strict/unfair
13.0 % Disrespectful

7.6% Doesn't explain
4.1% Poor discipline
2.8% Not liking children

What makes you happy at school?
62.8% Friendships
24.7% Particular subjects
5.9% Recognition of good work
4.3% Teaching methods

What makes you unhappy at school?
33.5% Bullying
24.9% Specific subjects
16.5% Unfairness
13.8% Falling out with friends

It is therefore very apparent that we can write as much as we like on IEPs about resources, teaching methods and number of hours of specialist/small group teaching but we still will not meet the student's needs unless some of our educators make some changes:

1. Educators need to adopt a kind, understanding, respectful, fair and creative attitude towards students and their work in order to provide a good 'climate' for learning.
   (Educators cannot adopt such behaviours unless they have a good understanding of the SpLD Profile conditions, have been trained in some effective strategies and have adequate breaks from students with challenging behaviour. The latter is exceptionally important in primary schools where classroom teachers/teaching assistants may get few, if any breaks from their class).
2. Educators who shout, are bad tempered, are too strict/unfair and disrespectful to students will not succeed in enabling them to learn.

Such teachers will only escalate classroom management problems when students are present who have a condition that causes difficult behaviour (e.g. Attention Deficits/ Autistic Spectrum Disorder). Senior Management Teams (SMTs) are likely to need to provide extra training and support for such staff. SMTs also need to recognise that such staff may be behaving in this way because they are under undue stress - many educators are being overworked at present.

3. Friendships are vitally important for student well-being. All too often our SpLD Profile students have few (if any) friends and may find keeping those friends difficult especially if self esteem is low, or if social skills are weak or if language/auditory processing difficulties are present. Educators need to:
    ● be on the look out for isolated students,
    ● manage classroom activities so that when group work is being done the student is not the 'last one chosen to make up the team',
    ● ensure that the student is seated beside someone who is not going to be unpleasant to the student.

4. Make sure that the student is not being bullied. People only bully the weak, those who cannot, or who fear, standing up for themselves. Therefore, all schools need to
    ● consider offering assertive courses to students who are regularly bullied,
    ● encourage the development of a buddying system so that the student is not isolated in the playground,
    ● be on the look out for verbal and physical bullying within the classroom. (Educators need to be aware that verbal bullying is as bad as physical bullying. In a secondary school it is especially easy for individual staff not to realise that a student is being verbally bullied in most of the lessons.)

5. Make sure that the student is not overworking. In Years 10 and 11 this can be achieved by reducing the number of GCSE subjects being studied by at least one subject and enabling the student to use the lessons freed up for private study.

General Index

Resource Index

50 Notes